AF589109

TESTIMONIALS

Nicole's superpower is honest, raw, and engaging reflection partnered with action, and thankfully she does not keep it to herself. Through this book she guides the reader to gain this same power in and for themselves. Every chapter is a new opportunity to be drawn to the table for a conversation, which is how it feels as you read. This is an invitation to change the conversations one has with oneself—the lies believed, the truths distorted, and the wounds that alter self-perception. Nicole "leans into her greatness," and we benefit greatly.

—W. J. Bryan Lewis

Reading *It's Not Me, It's You* felt like sitting across from a trusted friend who dared to say the quiet parts out loud—about survival, about shrinking, and about the long journey back to yourself.

Nicole's words hit me in a place I didn't realize needed tending. This book helped me name the unspoken ways I've carried imposter syndrome, especially in spaces where I've shown up fully competent, but not always fully confident. Her story gave me permission to stop minimizing my own experiences just to keep the peace or make others comfortable.

What stayed with me the most was her courage to face hard conversations and release relationships that no longer served her healing. It reminded me that it's okay to say: *This isn't healthy for me, and I deserve more.* There's something deeply liberating about watching another woman walk through fire and come out radiant with truth.

Nicole's framework of *Pain, Purpose, and Promise* isn't just a catchy title, it's a real-life roadmap for any woman who's ever questioned her worth, stayed too long, or silenced her own voice for the comfort of others. I saw my family on these pages. I saw my friends on these pages. I saw myself on these pages. And I left feeling a little more whole, a little more honest, and a lot more powerful.

—H. Pearson

It's Not Me, It's You is the kind of book that stops you mid-sentence and makes you say WOW! It's not a story of survival inasmuch as it is an act of reclamation. Nicole writes with the kind of honesty that doesn't require sympathy, instead it demands courage. She takes the hardest parts of her life and turns them into something fiercely useful. She moves from pain to power with brutal honesty and unflinching grace. It's raw without being reckless and real without the gloss of easy healing. It is a mirror for anyone who's ever questioned their worth, stayed too long or dimmed their own light to survive.

This book reminds us that strength doesn't come when we attempt perfection. It comes when we can stop apologizing for merely existing. This book will dare you to tell the truth about your own life. Do it.

—Loren Sanders
Author of *Empathy Is Not a Weakness*
and *Other Stories from The Edge*

Labels Be Gone

It's Not Me, It's You

TAKE THEIR LABELS OFF

It's Not Me, It's You

NICOLE LYNN MORRIS

For permission requests, contact Patrice Perkins at Creative Genius Law using the details below:

Patrice N Perkins
pperkins@creativegeniuslaw.com
171 N. Aberdeen Street, 4th Floor
Chicago, Illinois 60607

The opinions expressed by the Author are not necessarily those held by Publish Your Purpose.

Ordering Information: Quantity sales and special discounts are available on quantity purchases by corporations, associations, and others. For details, contact the author at nicole@labelsbegone.com.

Edited by: Anna Heim, David Aretha, Lily Capstick
Cover design by: Nelly Murariu
Typeset by: Medlar Publishing Solutions Pvt Ltd., India

Printed in the United States of America.

ISBN:979-8-88797-190-2 (hardcover)
ISBN:979-8-88797-191-9 (paperback)
ISBN:979-8-88797-192-6 (ebook)

Library of Congress Control Number: 2025912241

First edition, May 2026.

The information contained within this book is strictly for informational purposes. The material may include information, products, or services by third parties. As such, the Author and Publisher do not assume responsibility or liability for any third-party material or opinions. The publisher is not responsible for websites (or their content) that are not owned by the publisher. Readers are advised to do their own due diligence when it comes to making decisions.

Publish Your Purpose is a hybrid publisher of non-fiction books. Our mission is to elevate the voices often excluded from traditional publishing. We intentionally seek out authors and storytellers with diverse backgrounds, life experiences, and unique perspectives to publish books that will make an impact in the world. Do you have a book idea you would like us to consider publishing? Please visit PublishYourPurpose.com for more information.

LEGAL DISCLAIMER

This memoir is based on the author's recollections and interpretations of real events. Some names, locations, and identifying details have been changed to protect privacy. The views and opinions expressed are solely those of the author. Any resemblance to actual persons, living or dead, other than those intentionally portrayed, is purely coincidental.

DEDICATION

First and foremost this book is dedicated to me! The me that I had to be so that I could endure. The me that I had to be so that I could overcome. The me that has evolved to the place where I could turn my pain into purpose and that purpose into the promise of this book! I will stay looking in the mirror saying "I got you Cole!"

To my mom, my literal example of courage and womanhood, everything I am today is because of who you are and what you didn't let the world take from you. This too is YOUR Legacy.

To my husband, words would never do justice to articulate everything you are to me. Thank you for being the walking experience of unconditional love and support that I never knew I needed. Because of you, this project was birthed sooner and with a level of authenticity that the world needed. Of your many ripples, this will be one of the biggest.

To my babies, my "4Eva Why," my prayer is that my transparency, my courage, my truth, my strength, and my love sets you up to create the life you want to live. Know that you have the power to create and the power to choose. I love y'all and mama always got y'all!

CONTENTS

SECTION TWO

SECTION THREE

FOREWORD

It is my joy to introduce *It's Not Me, It's You: Take Their Labels Off* and its author, Nicole Morris. I met Nicole years ago in graduate school, and even then, her ambition, eagerness to learn, and unwavering support for others stood out. Over time, I came to think of her as my "bonus daughter," a role she earned through her resilience, determination, and quiet strength in the face of challenges.

Those qualities are not only what make Nicole remarkable; they are what make this book necessary. For years, I knew she had a message to share. When she finally told me she was writing, I was not surprised. What she has created here is more than a memoir—it is a conversation, a reckoning, and an invitation.

Nicole does not simply tell stories; she draws you into them. With honesty and vulnerability, she shows how imprints from childhood, professional pressures, and relationship dynamics can shape who we think we are, and how reclaiming our true identity requires unlearning, reflection, and courage. She invites you, the reader, to pause at pivotal moments, not just to witness her journey, but to examine your own.

This is what makes her work so powerful. You will see yourself in these pages . . . In the silences you've kept, the labels you've carried, and the moments when you longed to choose yourself but didn't. Nicole reminds us that doing so is more than survival. *It is at once a defiant act of reclamation, an intimate practice of listening within, and a simple habit of hearing your own truth above the world's noise.*

So I invite you: Don't just read this book. Enter into it. Let it stir your questions, your grief, your hope. Join the community that is stripping off everyone else's expectations and taking on the identity they choose.

Nicole signs her final words, "Yours in Courage." May that same courage meet you here, in these pages, as you begin your own work of unbecoming everything you never were.

LaConna Gowder

INTRODUCTION

"Maybe the journey isn't about becoming anything. Maybe it's about unbecoming everything that isn't really you, so that you can be who you were meant to be in the first place."

—Paulo Coelho

Psychologists call it **imprinting**. It is the process where we learn who we are. Or at least, who we think we are. In plain words: We get ideas of who we are at any point in life based on who and what is around us.

The people around us—their words, their energy, and even what they don't say—send subliminal messages about our worth. What we deserve. Who we are allowed to be. And even who we are **not** allowed to be.

Over time, those messages start to sink in. Some are truths worthy of building our lives around. Others are lies that we end up treating like the truth. We are largely unaware of these lies, yet they become the primary source of the limits we place on ourselves.

Imagine the imprints given to a child born into poverty with a drug-addicted father and a metaphysically battered mother. I was that child.

Even though my mother's natural and spiritual love gave me a strong foundation, my father's absence created the first cracks in my sense of self-worth. Not quite broken, but more like a hairline fracture. Even more dangerous because they are so easy to misdiagnose.

Psalm 51:5 says, "Behold, I was brought forth in iniquity, and in sin did my mother conceive me."

Iniquity, as it is used here, has several definitions, one of which is injustice. It reminds us that some of us are born into family stories, cycles, and systems that stamp us with limitations long before we even know what it means to *be*.

If we never stop to question where we got our ideas about who we are, or why we are the way we are, we risk spending our entire lives guided by **imprints** that never belonged to us.

This isn't a story about trauma, although a lot of that is in here.

It's also not an attempt to talk about the stereotypical Black American experience and its impact on people like me, although a lot of that is in here too.

It's much bigger than that!

It's about clarity.

It's about naming the labels we've all picked up, from family, from culture, from rejection, from the disappointments that can come daily, and having the courage to ask:

Do I still want to carry this?

This book is an open invitation to step inside some of the rawest and most vulnerable pieces of my life. I transparently share the process I walked through to identify the purpose in all the pain. To observe how I made sense of the mess and turned it into something I could *give back.*

And maybe . . . just maybe . . . in these pages you'll not only hear a reflection of my story, but find a spark for your own.

TAPED TATTERED PIECES

In my late twenties, I began to ask myself why I experienced life the way I did. On paper, I had achieved a lot; but beneath those accomplishments lived deep insecurity. I longed for a "lighter life," yet I had no idea how to break free from the cycles of trauma that kept repeating themselves.

The best way I can describe it is like this: My life felt like a sheet of paper torn into pieces, scattered on the floor, and trampled on by the weight of life. At the time, I was waiting for someone else to come along and put those pieces back together.

But one day, in a moment of reflection, I realized no one was coming. The paper was torn, and it was mine to mend. So, I chose to do the work. To gather the "pieces" and tape them back together, piece by piece. It wouldn't be perfect. Some pieces would still carry residual "dirt." But it would be intentional. And for the first time, I was determined to rebuild my life from the roots of how I saw myself.

I

THE FOUNDATIONAL LIE

One of my earliest memories, and maybe the most innocent, is of me sitting on a curb around the age of three or four, making mud pies.

And honestly? Back then (and even now) it was always the simple things that brought me joy. Dirt in my hands. Sun on my skin. No worries or fear. Just me, in my own little world.

Just "happy-go-lucky" presence and playing.

We were living in a big yellow building on 55th and Emerald, a tough neighborhood on the South Side of Chicago, though I didn't know that yet. My mom had just left my dad, though I didn't understand what that meant either.

What I *did* know was dingy green walls in our apartment, the crackling sound followed by the unforgettable smell of Spam frying on the stove (which I hated then and still do now), using chipped dishes, and having the stereotypically strong Black woman raising me and my older brother.

A mother who was "doing the best she could with what she had," and all the unspoken and subconscious essence that this kind of woman imparts.

I was a little girl lost in my own world . . . as it should've been.

Then, a shift.

A car began pulling in to the curb behind me. I didn't hear it. I didn't turn around. I didn't even know what a car really *was*, let alone that it could hurt me. And just before it reached me, someone, I don't know for certain who, grabbed me out of the way.

No yelling. No drama. Just movement.

And then . . . awareness.

Looking back now, I see that as a moment that began a negative imprint I still carry today, one that whispers the question: *Am I worthy of being protected?*

Pause & Reflect

When the World First Touched Us

My memory, sitting on a curb while lost in mud pies, and suddenly pulled out of harm's way, stays with me because it was the *first stain* on my previously blank canvas. When someone pulled me out of the way of that car, something small but powerful shifted.

This shift brought an awareness that the world wasn't really safe for me.

Maybe you have a moment like that too. Maybe it wasn't dramatic or loud.

Just an ever so slight shift that you can't quite name, but you know it happened.

Here's what I reflect on today:

- **I was a child likely being protected by another child.** My big brother, no older than seven or eight, was likely the one who saved me. A child guarding a child. In many families, that's how it goes.

  Who looked out for you when they were still learning to look out for themselves?

- **We lived in a place where danger was part of the daily background.** Not because anybody wanted that, but because surviving doesn't always leave room for "safety."

  Back then, I thought it was normal. Now? I know better.

What did you grow up believing was normal . . . until you saw it through adult eyes?

- **I sat with my back to danger, fully absorbed in play.** I wasn't being reckless; I was just being a kid. But the world I was in didn't have the safety nets kids deserve.

  Can you remember the moment you first felt vulnerable? The first time you realized the world might not be nice just because you were.

- **I remember Spam, not for the taste, but for what it represented.** That detail, salty, cheap survival food, lives clearly in my memory. Not because of the flavor, but because of what it *represented*: lack, compromise, and the quiet sacrifices my mother made to keep us going.

  What everyday thing from your past carries more emotional weight than it seems like it should?

This is about conscious awareness more than anything else.

My healing started when I went back to that first shift, that moment when life told me a lie about who I was—and even more impactfully, who I wasn't.

II

BLOODLINES AND IMPRINTS

Let me take a moment to tell you where I come from—not just names and locations, but the people, choices, and secrets that shaped my bloodline and the imprints it would leave.

In Black American families, especially, our stories aren't always clean or complete.

In my case, the paternal history that I do know I learned through "old folks' tales" on the rare occasions that I spent time with my father's family.

Some of it I've been able to verify; some of it not so much.

And yet, the imprints of what I do know make sense with who I am today.

My father's last name was Adams, which he took from his father—until I was writing this book, I wasn't sure if that was his real last name.

From what's been passed down, my great-grandmother was a mulatto woman who worked in a camera shop owned by a

White family during the Jim Crow era. Her skin tone gave her access that the typical Black American couldn't have.

That access came with both privileges and risks.

The story goes that the family's son started sneaking around with her while his parents were out to lunch. And from that—whatever it truly was—my grandfather was conceived.

Once she became pregnant, the family supposedly disappeared.

She raised my grandfather alone and would later marry a man who would affectionately be known as "Grandpa Frank." As I've been able to gather, "Frank" gave him a presence, an example, and an opportunity to explore his budding interests in electronics.

That detail of not being sure what my name really was might seem small. But names carry weight. They hold history. And when you don't know your name or have uncertain roots, it can shape how you do, or do not, see yourself.

Grandpa Frank was brilliant. He worked with his hands and had a small business—a repairman, maybe an electrician. I remember the shop he kept—full of TVs, all sorts of electronic devices, and, apparently, possibilities that my grandfather would explore.

My grandfather followed in his footsteps—mechanically gifted, smart, sharp. He served in the Navy and would later work on weapons systems that our nation uses today.

He met my grandmother, Mildred.

A chocolate brown woman with presence. My mother always described her as the full package: warm, graceful, brilliant. A homemaker and an incredible cook, yes—but she would also complete a bachelor's degree at Roosevelt University in Chicago.

Back when women like her weren't expected to show up in places like that, let alone excel.

From what I gather, both of my grandparents were revolutionists and unafraid to battle systems that they thought were unfair. That would explain quite a bit about me as well.

Although she had this drive, she and my grandfather agreed that the family came first. She stayed focused on raising their children. There was a focus on educational excellence and achievement.

She followed Dr. Spock's parenting methods—progressive for the time, centered around trust, emotional attentiveness, and giving children room to be themselves. My mom always joked that the method was a little "out there." But even so, I get the sense that my grandmother wanted to be tuned in, not just present. She was educated, intuitive, and, from what I've gathered, gentle but sharp. She valued connection. She believed in showing up.

Even though I had her for only a few short years, I felt that from her—even then.

Some of my earliest and most vivid memories are in her kitchen. I was about three. I remember the smell of soul food cooking, the warmth of the room, the soft yellow-colored walls in the spacious kitchen, and the little plastic apron she bought me—white with red trim and bright-colored fruit all over it. It had deep pockets too . . . it was made just for me.

While she cooked, she would help me practice writing my name on the chalkboard in the kitchen. It was more than play. It was learning. It was love. It was legacy.

She kept glass jars of candy on the credenza in the dining room—and I remember her hands, soft but steady, handing me my favorite: those sugar-coated orange slices.

To this day, I keep jars of snacks and mints around my house—little gestures of comfort, the way she offered them to me. I still gravitate toward vibrant, life-giving colors, like the ones on that apron.

And I see her in me when I show up strong in difficult spaces. Like when I stay grounded in rooms that weren't designed for me to succeed—just like she did when she earned her degree in a world that didn't give her permission to.

Her imprint on me was indelible. And she did all of that in just a handful of years.

What I didn't understand back then—couldn't have—was her sickness.

She died of cancer when I was still a toddler. And strangely, I don't remember there being much grief. No loud mourning. No dramatic goodbyes.

Unfortunately, when she passed, it wasn't just her that disappeared.

It was my connection to her side of the family. To my father. My grandfather. Her people. Their presence went with her.

To this day, I wonder:

What would life have been like if someone had stayed to hold us together after she left?

Even with so little time, her mark remains.

Pause & Reflect

When Legacy Outlives Time

My memory, sitting in my grandmother's kitchen, apron tied tight, chalk in hand, and being taught while she cooked, stays with me because it was one of the earliest examples of love that felt both ordinary and sacred.

A small moment and soft presence that would shape how I live, how I love, and how I show up.

She died when I was just a toddler. And after she passed, the people, the places, and the connection to her side of the family went with her.

It wasn't dramatic . . . I didn't notice it at the time. But it had a lasting imprint.

Maybe you've had an experience like that too.

Maybe someone shaped you deeply, even if they didn't stay long.

Maybe the grief came quietly, but the imprint stayed loud.

Here's what I still reflect on:

- **My grandmother's love was one of my first imprints.**

  I only had her until I was about three. And then . . . I didn't. But the way she showed up, the way she made space for me, left a mark that remains.

  Who left a loving mark on you, even if you barely had time together?

- **She was brilliant, beautiful, and bold, a trailblazer in her time.**

  She earned a degree from Roosevelt University when most Black women weren't even invited to try. That kind of courage runs in my blood, and I know I've inherited pieces of that spirit.

  What strengths do you carry that reflect someone close to you, even though you had limited time with them?

- **She was the glue, and when she left, things fell apart.**

  After her passing, I lost connection not just to her, but to the rest of her people. To my father. To his father. To their stories. All of it slipped away . . . drowned in silence and pain.

  Who held your family together? And what happened when they were no longer there to do it?

This isn't about sadness for what was lost.

It's about honoring what *remains*—the gestures, the memories, the pieces of them that live on in us.

My healing started when I realized I didn't have to forget her just because others let her fade.

Her love still lives in how I care for people. In the colors I'm drawn to.

In the jars of snacks I keep around the house.

Her legacy didn't disappear.

It took root . . . *in me.*

III

"SANTA CLAUS AIN'T REAL": MY FIRST EXTERNAL POWER STRUGGLE

At the time of my grandmother's passing, my father's crack addiction began to consume him. My mother could no longer tolerate it because the man who had been her rescuer and protector in their younger years had sometimes become her abuser under the influence of his addiction.

He had spiraled, and she wasn't going to let him take us down with him.

Because we were so poor, she got approved for Section 8 housing. We moved into a new building in the heart of Englewood, one of the most dangerous neighborhoods on the South Side of Chicago. But to her, it felt like a new beginning. She was hopeful. She was proud. I was around six or seven at the time.

I didn't have a concept of what made a neighborhood "good" or "bad." As a kid, life just was what it was.

Not long after we moved in, my older brother and I went outside to meet some of the neighborhood kids. I remember standing on a low bar in the yard, holding onto something overhead for balance as we talked. Somehow, we landed on the topic of Santa Claus.

I believed in him. My mom had made sure that even in the middle of our struggle, Christmas still felt magical. She couldn't afford a lot of gifts, but she told stories and played games all centered around Santa. She made something out of nothing. That was enough for me to believe that Santa was real.

But the girl next door, and the boy with her, weren't buying it. They shut it down immediately and told me that Santa wasn't real—no way, no how. I pushed back. I knew what I believed.

Then, out of nowhere, *flop*—I hit the ground.

The girl had pushed me off the bar. No warning, no hesitation. Just like that.

I wasn't used to fighting. I didn't expect it, especially not over something like this. I felt confused, embarrassed, and, honestly . . . a little heartbroken. Why did she care so much about what *I* believed?

I went back inside, shaken. My mom, of course, reassured me. Told me Santa was still real. But something in me had already shifted.

That moment stuck with me. It was the first time I remember someone outside of me making me question something I truly believed in. A moment where my innocence met resistance. The belief was still there, but it was no longer untouched.

It was the beginning of learning how the world can chip away at what feels pure, even when all you're trying to do is hold on to a little magic.

Pause & Reflect

When Innocence Unknowingly Entered an Unsafe Place

My memory, standing on a low bar in front of our new apartment, balancing myself while talking about Santa Claus, stays with me because it was the first time I realized the world could push back. **Literally**.

One moment, I was sharing something I believed in.

The next, I was on the ground.

It wasn't just about Santa.

It was about the shock of realizing I could be physically hurt without cause.

It wasn't a big scene . . . Just a disagreement followed by a push and a fall.

My confidence also took a fall that day. It was something I hadn't even known was holding steady.

Maybe you have had a moment like that too, a quiet nudge from the world that made you see yourself, or your surroundings, in a whole new way. Maybe it wasn't loud either. But it stuck.

Here's what I still reflect on:

- **I was in a new environment, and I didn't know the rules. I didn't know what "safe" looked like there.**

  I didn't even realize I could be vulnerable.

  Have you ever entered a new space not knowing what it would require from you? And then it showed you in a not-so-pleasant way?

- **I wasn't looking for conflict.**

  I was just being me, wide-eyed, open-hearted, and speaking what I believed.

  Can you recall a time when you were just showing up as yourself and the world decided that was too much?

- **The confusion hurt a little more than the fall.**

  The sting of wondering if I had done something wrong just by believing in something good.

  What moment first made you question yourself, not because you were wrong, but because someone else made you feel like you were?

- **I believed in Santa not just because I was a kid, but because my mother worked hard to keep magic alive.** Even in struggle, she gave me light.

  What belief did someone protect for you, even when the world made it hard?

When reflecting on this, I realized that sometimes healing begins by revisiting the moment we first started to doubt ourselves.

The moment a piece of our innocence got redefined as "naïve."

The moment the world handed us a question where we had once known certainty.

I carried that doubt for a long time.

But today, I remind myself of a deeper truth:

I didn't deserve the push, and I never had to stop believing in magic to survive.

IV

I THOUGHT IT WAS MY FAULT

CONTENT ADVISORY

The following section includes a depiction of sexual violence. While it is written with care and intention, please take the space you need before reading. Your well-being matters.

His name was "Matt."

Looking back, he was probably what most people would've called the neighborhood bum. Every hood had one, a man everybody knew, nicknamed, and ignored. He seemed harmless . . . until he wasn't.

After we moved into the new place, my mom found out that one of our neighbors had a home daycare. It worked out perfectly.

My brother and I were technically too young to be home alone, and Ms. Smith's place was really close.

Ms. Smith fit every warm, no-nonsense "Big Mama" stereotype you could imagine: a thick, dark-skinned woman with silver hair, a house dress, and sagging breasts that seemed to stretch to her stomach. She could cook like a dream and cuss you out in the same breath. That was my babysitter.

She also cared for her disabled relative, Barry, who stayed in what used to be the dining room. His big medical bed sat right near one of the two entrances to the bathroom. Barry and I shared the same birthday. That little fact always made me smile.

Ms. Smith didn't work a regular job, but she hustled hard. She raised chickens in the backyard, sold icy cups, and watched her soap operas and *The People's Court* religiously. She was part of the rhythm of that neighborhood.

I remember wanting so badly to go to the penny candy lady's house, a journey that involved sneaking out the back, cutting through an alley, across a vacant lot, through two gangways, and going up a back porch. It only took a quarter or two for a good trip, but most days we didn't have it. And I knew better than to ask.

So, one day, I went rummaging through Ms. Smith's cabinet, hoping to quietly "borrow" some change. I don't even remember if I found any. What I do remember is what came after.

I was kneeling on Ms. Smith's ottoman, watching *The People's Court*, when I felt it . . . that uncomfortable, something-isn't-right feeling that we often don't know how to name. I turned around.

Matt was lying on the floor behind me. Flat on his back, knees spread, eyes locked on my six-year-old body.

Something in me froze. I stood up and left the room. Quickly, quietly.

Later, I went to use the bathroom, the one with the two doorways, and as I was finishing, Matt came in from Barry's entrance. I had just fastened my pants when he stepped toward me.

"I saw you stealing that money today," he said.

"Unless you pull your pants down and sit on my face, I'm gon tell."

Petrified.

That's the only word for what I felt.

My thoughts collided: *I got caught . . . I'm in trouble . . . I did something bad . . .* ***I deserve this***.

Shame rose faster than my body could react. I began fumbling with the top button of my pants, believing this was the consequence of my actions. That somehow, I'd brought this on myself.

But then, another shift.

Some small, powerful voice in me said **no**.

I didn't have the words. I didn't have the tools.

But I had the instinct.

I began slowly shaking my head "no" and took tiny, trembling steps backward, until I found the other exit and ran.

I didn't tell.

Not because I wasn't scared, but because I thought I was *equally guilty*.

I'd gone looking for money. I had "sinned." He had caught me. And in my six-year-old mind, that made what he did *my fault* too.

That was the beginning of a long, internal war.

A simmering belief that I was somehow damaged. That I had invited harm. That worthlessness had a home in me.

That moment didn't just scare me. It imprinted me. And seemingly, it was one of my own making.

Pause & Reflect

When Guilt Took the Mic

I didn't tell.

Not because I didn't know it was wrong.

But because I believed I was wrong too.

The shame didn't start with what he did; it started with what *I thought I did.* I had gone looking for change. That small act, driven by childhood want, felt like a moral failure in my six-year-old mind. So when he cornered me, demanded something unthinkable, and threatened me with exposure, I believed I was somehow to blame.

This is how silence starts.

This is how guilt becomes a script.

This is how power gets quietly taken and quietly surrendered.

Here's what I think about today when unpacking this:

- **My judgment of myself was brutally inflexible.**

  I didn't even consider that his actions were the true violation. My mind immediately went to *my* wrongdoing. I didn't even give myself space, in my own spirit, to feel like a victim.

  How early did you learn to be hard on yourself? So hard that you forgot how to protect yourself?

- **That judgment became a pattern.**

  Whenever something harmful was done to me, I muted myself. I replayed the same message: *You shouldn't have . . . You made it happen . . . You don't get to speak up.*

  What was the first lie you believed that made you feel as if your voice didn't matter?

- **Because I blamed myself, I couldn't see the injustice.**

  I didn't tell, not just because I was scared, but because I had already absorbed the idea that I deserved it. That pattern of self-blame didn't protect me. It kept me exposed.

  How many times have you kept quiet not because you were okay, but because you thought you were the problem?

This moment showed me how children internalize guilt before they ever understand power.

It showed me how easily silence can sometimes feel like the best choice.

And how quickly survival can become a strategy that costs us our authentic voice.

But here's the truth I keep returning to:

I didn't do it to myself.
He did it.

And today, I honor that little girl by saying out loud what she didn't feel safe to say:

You were not wrong. You were just a child. You deserved protection, not punishment.

V

THE BEGINNING OF CHASING REJECTION

One thing about my mother: if she believed the sky was available to her, she was going to reach for it. She never let herself be confined to what she saw or what she had. Even though we were planted in some of the roughest neighborhoods on Chicago's South Side, she'd load us into one of her raggedy cars and drive through the suburbs, saying, *"This is how you want to live."*

She was planting seeds.

In the summer of 1989, our apartment in the Gresham neighborhood was broken into. We suspected it was someone in the neighborhood and that was the final straw for her. She found a place in the south suburbs that accepted her Section 8 voucher, and by the fall, we were moving in. Just in time for school.

It wasn't exactly culture shock. But it was different. *Sharply* different.

If we hadn't already known we were poor, we knew once we moved there. There were no corner stores with bars on the windows. No overgrown lots or crumbling buildings. No "Matts" wandering the block or kids flipping on dirty mattresses in the alley. Just manicured lawns and two-parent households. Quiet streets and kids with name-brand shoes. People who seemed to have done life "right."

The difference wasn't just visual. It was felt. It was a subliminal echo of the *not enough* message that had been nestling its way into my psyche since the imprint on the curb.

I remember my first day of fourth grade in my new school. Everything was structured, almost ceremonial. We lined up outside on the playground, then again outside our classrooms, greeting each teacher with a formal "Good morning, Mrs. So-and-so" before we were allowed to enter. It felt . . . official. Almost like I was preparing to serve in some leadership role.

While most kids my age were probably just settling into school routines, I had already seen and felt more than most. The trauma I carried, from Matt and other things I didn't yet have language for, shaped how I viewed myself. I was already carrying the question: *Am I enough?*

I remember noticing a boy in class, one I thought was the cutest thing walking. We sat on opposite sides of the room. I kept hoping he'd notice "the new girl." He didn't. Not even when I started growing boobs. *Lol.*

I can laugh when I think about it now. But it says a lot.

At nine or ten years old, I wasn't just looking for a crush. I was already looking to feel *wanted.* I didn't know how to say it yet, but what I wanted was to feel seen. To be enough. Just as I was.

That feeling followed me. Through grade school. Into early church life. I'd find myself falling for boys who never saw me the same the way I saw them. I was poor. I was considered chubby. My hair wasn't always styled as nicely as the other girls. And more than all of that, I was already struggling with self-worth.

Moving to a "better" neighborhood didn't erase those things. It just put them under a brighter light.

And in that light, I started making internal trades—my voice, my boundaries, my self-esteem—all in exchange for being accepted.

What I didn't realize then was that stepping into a nicer zip code didn't magically grant me a "better life."

Instead, it heightened my awareness of what I felt that I lacked and deepened the lie that I had to *earn* acceptance in the first place.

Pause & Reflect

When Labels Start to Stick

We don't always notice the first time someone names us something we never agreed to. Such as . . .

"Too big." "Too poor." "Too much." "Not enough."

We just know it lands.

And then, little by little, it starts to stick.

Here's what I still reflect on:

- **I'd internalized so many labels that were never mine to carry.**

  Most of them weren't said with intention, just off-handed comments, teasing, little digs dressed up as "jokes." But over time, I absorbed them as truth. Not because they *were* true, but because I heard them so often I didn't know how to push them off.

  What label(s) did you adopt that didn't actually belong to you under the guise of a joke or some other form of supposed light-heartedness?

- **My trauma made me more vulnerable to the lies.**

  The wounds I hadn't spoken about, the ones I didn't even fully understand, made me more open to believing the worst about myself. If someone else said I wasn't enough, I didn't question it. I *already* felt like I wasn't.

  Did you have a time when your unhealed hurt made it easier to believe what others said about you?

- **I wore the trauma well.**

  I didn't "look" like I was hurting, not in the ways people expect. I smiled. I laughed. I showed up.

  But underneath it all, I was battling shame, silencing myself, and had a constant need to be accepted.

  *What part of you have you hidden so well that even **you** started to forget it needed care?*

The hard part about early labels is that we don't just carry them; we begin to live by them.

The truth I know today is: We have the power to rename ourselves.

Healing begins when we start to separate who we were labeled as from who we actually are.

VI

"PO' FAT CHILD"

My battle with weight has been a quiet thread running through my life for as long as I can remember. It traces all the way back to those early years on 62nd & Normal.

Looking back now, my body was actually pretty average for a little girl. But the way people casually joked about my "big belly" or "thick legs" made me feel anything but normal.

And it wasn't just at home; it followed me everywhere.

A constant reminder that I wasn't measuring up to something I didn't fully understand yet.

That attention made me self-conscious. Hypercritical. Until very recently, I can't recall having a healthy relationship with the mirror from the neck down. I didn't like what I saw, no matter what size I was.

And the belly, that belly, always felt like the sad, stubborn evidence of something wrong with me.

In my new neighborhood, I formed what I thought were friendships. But looking back, we were mostly a cluster of kids from complicated households sharing space, survival tactics, and unspoken pain in a row of aging apartment buildings.

The comments about my body didn't stop in the suburbs. They just changed voices. I remember trying to put myself on a "diet" once, a boiled egg and a cup of shredded cheese. That was it. I was probably around nine or ten. I didn't know anything about real nutrition, but I knew "eating less" was the rule. At least that's what the '80s taught us. That "diet" maybe lasted a day. Maybe. *Lol.*

Like always, money was tight. Section 8 kept a roof over our heads, but there wasn't room for extras—not candy, not chips, not soda. And yet, I still wanted what every kid wanted: a snack to feel normal.

The clerk at the corner gas station seemed to get that. On days I didn't have money, which was most days, she'd sometimes let me "pay later," pretending I had a tab. I'd fake-offer to pay her back, and she'd play along like I really would. We both knew I wouldn't. But she gave me that tiny sliver of dignity anyway.

One day, I went in like usual, picking out my snacks with no real plan to pay. Just as I was checking out, my "friend" came in behind me. We hadn't walked to the store together, and I hadn't wanted to announce I didn't have money. Before I could say anything, they stepped up, pulled out their wallet, and paid for my things.

Then they turned to the clerk and said, loud enough for everyone to hear, *"Sometimes I have to help my poor friend out."*

It landed like a slap.

Yes, it was *partially* true. We didn't have extra money for snacks.

However, that this declaration was made to the one adult who had quietly protected my dignity all this time felt more like exposure than help.

It worked.

In that moment, I felt the sting of layered shame: over my body, over my lack, and now, over being pitied by someone who only wanted to look good at my expense.

That memory stuck. Not because of the snacks. But because it marked another moment where I learned that trust could be fragile, especially with people who claim to care for you. I started to connect my worth to what I didn't have. I started to watch what people gave me . . . and if they used it to make me feel small.

And maybe that's what weight became for me over time, not just something I carried physically, but the emotional evidence of every time someone made me feel "less than."

Pause & Reflect

The First Cut Is Unnoticed

It's easy to downplay childhood moments like these.

It's just candy.

It's just a joke.

It's just a friend, or someone close, being . . . "honest."

But sometimes, what we shrug off as "small" in the moment becomes the soil for how we see ourselves over a lifetime.

Here's what I reflect on today:

- **People don't always mean harm, but that doesn't mean they don't cause it.**

  The comments about my weight may have been meant as jokes. Casual. Playful. But they rooted themselves in my spirit anyway. And they grew into a lifelong struggle with how I saw myself from the neck down.

  What words were spoken to you "lightly" that landed heavy and stayed?

- **Embarrassment can be a teacher, not just about ourselves, but about others.**

  That day in the gas station wasn't just about snacks. It was my first real glimpse into someone showing me who they were, and me not knowing what to do with that information.

Like Maya Angelou said: *"When someone shows you who they are, believe them."*

If I'd had that wisdom back then, I could've saved myself a lot of emotional detours.

What was the moment you realized someone you trusted wasn't actually safe, and what did you do with that truth?

- **Not every act of generosity is kind.**

  My "friend" paid for my snacks. In exchange, I felt like I repaid them with my dignity. That moment taught me that sometimes people give only to gain, and will do so at your expense.

  Have you ever been "helped" in a way that made you feel the opposite of supported? If so, where did you place the emotions that it stirred up?

We don't always realize the first time our trust is fractured.

We just remember the sting.

But now? We get to notice.

And we get to tell that younger version of ourselves:

You weren't crazy. That really did hurt. And you didn't deserve it.

VII

#METOO

CONTENT ADVISORY

The following section includes a depiction of sexual violence. While it is written with care and intention, please take the space you need before reading. Your well-being matters.

Eighth grade started out like every other school year. By the end of it, though, the spirit of sexual trauma that "Matt" had tried to visit on me a few years earlier would fully manifest itself at the hands of a young male classmate one day after school.

That rejection that I'd been chasing caught up with me. One day during the school day, a group of kids found ourselves having some free time and freedom to move about the building.

We ended up in the girls' locker room. As validation chasing would have it, I ended up letting my future perpetrator touch me inappropriately. I don't know what I was thinking or why because I didn't even like him.

Fast-forward to the next day or so, when I stayed after school for an activity. For some reason, he was still on school grounds then too. I'd gone back to the same area of the building from the day before, and he wanted to pick up where we'd left off. I was no longer interested in doing whatever that was.

He decided that wasn't acceptable and began to try to force me to kiss him. I've never been a shrinking violet or pushover, so we began to wrestle. I remember him pulling me back near some lockers and me being surprised that he was overpowering me. To give myself some leverage, I grabbed the lockers so I could pull myself forward. I pulled so hard that they nearly fell on us. Seeing this, I let them go, and he was able to pull me into a small corner space.

I remember having the thought "this is really happening to me" and freezing up as he pulled my elastic-waisted pants down with one hand while trying to force his other hand on my vagina. I had one last fight in me and pushed back against him, saying "No," and he began to yank on my pubic hairs. I don't remember what he was saying, but within seconds he'd forced himself into me and began thrusting. It seemed like just a few seconds before he quickly yanked himself away from me, like he had orgasmed by surprise. I was able to get away.

I left the building, on the opposite side of where I normally would go to walk home, and was completely discombobulated. I was processing what had just happened. Some of the questions floating around my head were: "Did that just happen?" "Did he cum in me?" "How did I get there?" WTF?!

He chased me down. Talking to me, trying to convince me that he hadn't raped me. I remember us going back and forth. I told him I was going to the police because I had told him no. His reply: "They're going to think I raped you." I said, "You did."

I went home, told my mom, and we went to the police.

The police told me I'd lied. They told me I was going to put him in jail and made it about me hurting him. They wrote out a statement for me recanting the accusation, and I signed it.

Damn.

I would learn the next week that this boy had done this to another female classmate before eighth grade. Years later, he tried to do something similar to a friend and was successful in doing it to a neighbor.

WHAT THE FUCK?!

Pause & Reflect

When Trauma Temporarily Rewrites the Story

There's something that happens in moments like these, when your body is violated and your mouth is covered.

You start trying to make sense of it with a framework that was never yours to begin with.

You ask yourself questions that have no business being yours to carry:

Was it my fault?

Did I lead him on?

Should I have fought harder?

Here's what I reflect on today:

- **No matter what I did before, I didn't give permission for *that*.**

  Letting someone touch me once didn't mean I owed them anything else. Going back to the same room didn't mean I signed up for violence. There was no contract. No consent. No excuse.

  When have you blamed yourself for something someone else chose to do?

- **My need to feel seen put me in harm's way, but that doesn't make the harm my fault.**

  I was hungry for validation. That's real. And that hunger led me into a situation I didn't know how to navigate. But his decision to cross a boundary wasn't my doing.

What have you called a "mistake" that was really a coping mechanism for unhealed wounds?

- **I've never been the same, but I'm still here.**

  That moment marked me in a way that no amount of healing can erase. But I no longer carry it in silence. I speak it, I name it, I reclaim the space it tried to take.

  What shifted in you after **your** *defining moment, and what truth are you ready to say out loud about it?*

This isn't about blame. This is about truth.

And telling the truth, in full rawness, holding nothing back, is how I began to loosen the grip that moment tried to have on my life.

VIII

THE CURSE OF COMPARTMENTALIZATION

High school is blurry for me.

Not because nothing happened, but because *too much* did.

I was too busy chasing *something*. What it was then, I didn't know.

After the rape, the people who were supposed to protect me failed, hard.

- The **police** told me I was lying. That I'd ruin his life if I didn't take back the accusation.
- My **father**, who hadn't been present for most of my life, showed up just long enough to yell at me based on what the police told him.
- My **principal** told me I wouldn't be allowed to participate in **my** eighth-grade graduation. Because I'd been raped.

Blow after blow after blow.
And I didn't deserve any of it.
But I internalized all of it.

We were always financially poor.

My mom made magic out of nothing. Rich in love, resourceful beyond measure, but money was always tight.

By thirteen, I had my first job, filing papers and doing janitorial work at my old grammar school.

By sixteen, I was working real hours and real jobs.

I paid rent to my mom. Bought my own school clothes and supplies.

Getting my hair done was a luxury. Name-brand clothes were for other kids.

I always felt behind.

And that feeling, of never catching up, turned into a chase.

At the time, I thought I was chasing money.

What I know now is that I was chasing *validation*.

I became a high-functioning, high-performing, emotionally disconnected machine.

- Honors student
- Part-time job

- Sports
- Friends
- Smiles

All while carrying trauma that I didn't have time to process.

I didn't realize how deeply the rape had bruised my spirit.

I didn't realize the quiet messages of worthlessness I had ingested, and how they showed up every time I pushed harder just to be *enough*.

The busier I stayed, the less I had to feel.

I buried my voice under responsibility.

I told myself I just needed to "finish."

In that chase, I doubled down on doubting myself.

I disregarded my own instincts in favor of what other people liked about what I was doing.

I believe that the people around me—adults, teachers, institutions—must know better than I did.

And the mistrust was *loud* . . . I just couldn't hear it.

I had compartmentalized myself into numbness.

Achievement became my armor.

Overextension became my currency.

Presence, especially with myself, was a gift that I didn't think to ask for.

This survival mode followed me into adulthood.

- I stayed in a toxic marriage that drained me emotionally, psychologically, and financially.
- I aligned myself with organizations that loved my gifts but offered no reciprocity.
- I maintained friendships that required my labor, yet gave little in return.

And I justified the imbalance with productivity.
I told myself I was okay because I was "accomplishing things."
But the truth?
I was depleting myself and calling it purpose.

Reflection didn't come quickly.

But piece by piece, I started to recognize the cost of the chase:

That in striving to be enough, I kept abandoning myself.

And eventually, I realized: Survival may have shaped me, but it didn't have to define me.

Pause & Reflect

When Your Silence Nurtures Your Survival

Some traumas don't explode.

They just unfold quietly, and then get buried even quieter.

No one talks about them.

No one checks in.

No one calls them what they are.

And so you learn to keep going.

To move forward.

To survive with a wound no one acknowledges, not even you.

Here's what I still reflect on:

- **The trauma happened, and we all just moved on.**

  No counseling. No school intervention. No emotional triage.

  It was as if my rape was a minor inconvenience to the adults around me.

  #normalizedneglect

  What have you experienced that should have been met with care, but was met with . . . nothing?

- **I didn't even know the rape was traumatic.**

  How could I have?

  No one told me what trauma looked like.

  No one told me what to expect, emotionally, mentally, physically.

So when I started feeling heavy, confused, disconnected, I didn't name it as harm.

I just thought something else was wrong with *me.*

When did you first realize that what you experienced ***wasn't normal****, even if everyone acted like it was?*

- **I hid behind performance.**

I stayed busy. I excelled. I pushed myself hard.

Because if I was doing well, I must be doing *fine*, right?

I didn't ignore the trauma.

I ignored *myself.*

#ignoringmyself

What parts of your pain have you tried to outrun with excellence or some other habit?

Sometimes, our deepest wounds wear masks.

And sometimes, the mask looks like a gold star.

But healing begins when we stop performing and start *noticing.*

Noticing what was lost.

What was buried.

What we're finally ready to reclaim.

FIGHTING GHOSTS TO CHASE ILLUSIONS

As it turns out, human beings do not merely carry the weight of psychological imprints. We also accumulate hormonal imprints over time, among likely several other forms of imprinting that science is only beginning to fully understand.

Now, consider the profound effect of experiencing psychological, chemical, and hormonal imprints simultaneously. The compounded impact of these imprints becomes even more significant when they occur during a developmental stage in life, particularly during a period when the brain is not only at its peak capacity for memory formation but is also still undergoing critical phases of growth.

Yeah . . . that's a stereotypical "first love" experience.

"The hormonal interactions are imprinted in the sensory areas of the brain at a time when the neurological developments we are experiencing are forming who we are as individuals."[1]

Now . . . sprinkle this with a little trauma bonding and you'll get my first experience with love.

---

[1] Ross Pomeroy, "Why First Love Has Such a Powerful Hold on Us, According to Psychology," *Big Think*, July 10, 2024, https://bigthink.com/neuropsych/psychological-first-love/.

I

MY FIRST (TOXIC) LOVE

There are two things I will never forget about my first love: 1) the first time we met, and 2) the way my soul was absolutely shattered when we broke up. Especially the part where he seemed to take pleasure in causing me pain. This would be one of the most significant mind fucks of my life—and it would absolutely shape the next ten to twenty years of my life.

It was the summer before senior year when I met my first real boyfriend.

And by "real," I mean the kind of relationship that swallows you whole. I was a damaged, compartmentalized, overachieving coper—ripe for the illusion of love that looked and felt right on paper.

He checked every box I'd been taught to care about: smart, articulate, attractive, employed, college-bound. We looked cute together. I mean, what else is a teenage girl looking for?!

Within weeks, we were all in—hard, fast, and, in my mind, forever.

The connection was intense. The orgasms were too.

In hindsight, the physical high blurred any clarity I might've had. I didn't know how to separate affection from attention, chemistry from compatibility.

That's the trick of trauma bonding: the nervous system confuses emotional intensity for safety. When you grow up learning to chase love in unstable places, your barometer for what's "real" is often completely off.

Senior year was a blur of school, part-time work, college applications, and daydreams scribbled in the margins of my AP English notebook, where I practiced writing his last name after mine.

I was doing the absolute most—National Honor Society, full scholarship, top 10 percent of my class—and yet I had almost zero emotional bandwidth.

And at the center of my emotional world?

Him.

What I didn't realize at the time was that my ambition and my attachment were both being fueled by the same thing: unprocessed trauma.

I was always striving—for love, for success, for proof that I mattered.

The hunger came from years of lack, from watching my mother hustle with dignity, and from surviving a rape that no one, including me, had ever dealt with.

So when he started pulling back—by skipping school, getting high, and drifting away—I filled in the blanks with fantasy.

I convinced myself he was just "going through something," that he was deep, brilliant, and misunderstood.

But the truth was, he was just being a regular eighteen-year-old—while I was sprinting toward a version of adulthood he was never built for.

We used to talk about college, about our future. I believed him.

Everyone saw the shift coming. Everyone but me.

The more distant he became, the more desperate I was to hold on.

I twisted myself into something I thought he'd want. I shrank parts of myself just to stay relevant in his story.

What I didn't know then (but know deeply now) is that I wasn't chasing him. I was chasing the validation I thought his love could offer.

That's the hook of trauma bonding: Your nervous system mistakes familiarity for safety. The highs and lows mimic the chaos you've known. You confuse survival mode with intimacy. And you fight for the pain because it feels like home.

I wasn't just afraid of losing him; I was afraid of what losing him would say about me.

That I wasn't enough. That I was disposable. That maybe love really wasn't mine to have.

Eventually, I began to let go.

Slowly . . . I stopped thinking about him every day. I stopped waiting.

And then, just as the fog began to lift, I got a page on my beeper with our old "I love you" code. My heart flipped. Maybe . . . ?

No.

What followed was twenty-four hours of, what felt like, coordinated harassment.

There were multiple phone calls from various people . . . sometimes everyone talking at me all at once. It felt like I was being mocked for having a broken heart. At one point, one of the callers made it known that they were trying to have a baby. Apparently, I was just a fling and nothing serious.

I couldn't believe it. After everything we'd been through, after all the "time and history" we shared, I was reduced to a throwaway line? No way was I accepting that and I offered to meet them in person the next day.

I was going to "prove" that I mattered and brought every piece of "evidence" I thought I had.

Of course, the meetup never happened.

To this day, I still don't know why that happened to me.

Back then, it gutted me . . . Today, I see it for what it was: my emotional rock bottom.

It was the day I realized that no one was coming to save me: not from the heartbreak, not from the ghosts in my head, and not from the lie that being loved meant I was worthy.

So I did the only thing I could think of . . . I started journaling. I tried to live like a "normal" nineteen-year-old. I dated. I smiled. I functioned.

But I was still leading with wounds, not wisdom.

And that set the stage for nearly two decades of misaligned connections—choosing people based not on who they were, but on who I desperately needed them to be.

I was looking for love, all kinds, in all the wrong places.

Pause & Reflect

Ghosts, Illusions, and the Mirror We Avoid

First love has a way of imprinting on us, especially when it intersects with unhealed trauma. What we call "falling" is often clinging. What we call "forever" is often familiarity. That cycle of craving, loss, and return can feel like passion . . . until we realize it's just pain in disguise.

This wasn't just a story about *him*. It was about me.

And maybe it's about you too.

Take a breath. Sit with this:

- **Fighting ghosts and chasing illusions** was all about my misinformed thoughts about myself.

  What false beliefs about yourself have you carried into love, work, or self-worth?

- **Fighting ghosts and chasing illusions** didn't just show up in love. It was in *every area* of my life. Work, friendship, ambition. Always running. Always reaching.

  Where else in your life have you been performing for validation or chasing something that doesn't serve you?

- **The only one who could break the cycle was me.** Not him. Not time. Not closure. Me.

  What cycle in your life is waiting for you to be the one to interrupt it—on purpose?

How many cycles in your life are just misinformed stories featuring different characters? What illusions are you still chasing because of who you were told you had to be?

Naming it is where the healing begins. Reclaiming it is where the freedom lives.

II

WHAT IS THIS MARRIAGE THING ANYWAY?

By nineteen, the residue was thick. I didn't know to call it trauma. I didn't know what to call what I was carrying—I just knew it was heavy. But it was also normal . . . just how life was. Looking back now, here's some of what I had in my emotional backpack:

- **Parental abandonment.** Where *was* my father? Why is one of my most vivid memories of him the time he stole my Christmas present to support his addiction?
- **Violence at home.** And I don't mean sibling roughhousing. Sometimes, both my brother and my mom would unleash on me physically.

- **Unaddressed rape.** I just kept going. Went to school like nothing happened. Didn't pause. Didn't process. Just kept going.
- **Deep self-hatred.** I was judge, jury, and executioner for myself. My inner dialogue? ***Relentless***. The most dangerous conversations I've ever had were the ones between me and me—and I was off to a terrible start.

And then, in the middle of all that pain, I met him.

I still remember the first time I saw my ex-husband with a kind of odd fondness. He'd become my next "serious" relationship. The one I'd stay in for nearly two decades.

I was nineteen and had just landed a job as a bank teller. This particular branch opened at 7 a.m., which meant we had to be there by 6:45 a.m. One morning, I pulled into the lot and saw him arrive right after me, followed by our supervisor.

He stepped out of a small red car, dressed like it was Sunday morning at a Black Baptist church. Fresh-pressed shirt, slacks, tie, shoes polished to a mirror shine, sunglasses, and all. The sun hit him just right from behind, making the whole scene feel like something out of a movie.

At the time, I didn't really know him beyond the fact that his name sat on my job application as a reference. Meeting him in person for the first time, all I could think was, *"Okay, he's kinda smooth."*

We worked together for a while, getting to know each other like people do in those early adulthood years, through observation, small talk, and a little too much personal oversharing. He struck me as kind. Stable. Went to church. Loved his nephews. Kept a job. Kept a crease in his pants. He seemed like a good guy.

And "nice"? That wasn't something I was used to associating with men in my life.

We started dancing around the idea of something more. Then one winter day, after a long shift, he went out ahead of me, cleaned off my car, and shoveled a path from the office to my driver's side door. That was it for me. That was the moment I decided I was done with the dance.

I made the first move. I told him it was time. (Side note: the fact that I had to make the first move should've been the first red flag, but . . . *he was nice*—and nice was new.)

Fast-forward about a year. We dated for six months and then decided to get married.

What the fuck was I and anybody around me thinking?!

Pause & Reflect

When Pain Makes the Choice

It's easy to look back with clarity. Hindsight always has 20/20 vision. But when I think back, I realize that I was nineteen, worn down, and reaching for anything that felt like stability:

I didn't choose him from a place of wholeness.

I chose him from the ache.

Here's what I've come to understand:

- **I let my pain, not my love of self, make the marital choice for me.**

  I didn't choose love. I chose *relief*.

  What decisions in your life were made to escape pain instead of embrace healing?

- **I looked past the red flags because I was too busy fighting ghosts.**

  I wasn't listening to my intuition. I was arguing with my insecurities and trying to prove I was enough.

  Have you ever silenced your inner voice just to prove something to someone else?

- **Yes, I was smart. Yes, I had potential. Yes, I had a good head on my shoulders.**

  And still, I got it wrong.

  Can you name a time you confused being capable with being clear?

So let me ask you:

Have you ever made a big life decision from a place of pain instead of power?

What would it look like to forgive yourself for that?

And better yet, what would it look like to make your next big decision(s) from a healed place?

III

UMMM . . . SPELL "BUDGET"

As it turned out, choosing the wrong partners wasn't the only area where I made decisions based on my pain.

Money was another one.

Growing up, we didn't have a lot. My mom was resourceful, and we never went without love, but we definitely went without luxury. There were no consistent trips to the hair or nail salon. No designer labels. Meanwhile, many of my suburban classmates lived lives that were quite the opposite—fresh hairstyles and name-brand everything.

I always felt like the poor, dingy duck.

By thirteen, I had my first W2 job through a state-funded youth employment program. And outside of the practical obligations, like helping to pay rent and buying school supplies, it shouldn't be hard to guess where the rest of my check went.

Every dollar not planned for went toward one mission: **buy the things my mom couldn't.**

By eighteen, I was working at a department store and handing my whole paycheck right back to the same place in exchange for temporary confidence. Retail therapy became my numbing agent. I spent myself into short-lived moments of happiness, trying to dress over the sense of not being "enough" I carried inside.

On the surface, I looked responsible, even impressive:

- College student with a full-ride scholarship
- Bought my first car on my own
- Paid bills and even contributed rent to my mom

But underneath all that achievement?

I was drowning in financial dysfunction.

By twenty, I had purchased my first brand-new car.

By twenty-one, I was married and had bought my first home.

I was **checking every box** on the adulting list . . . while bleeding out financially behind the scenes.

On the flip side . . .

By twenty-two, that brand-new car was repossessed.

By twenty-three, I'd experienced my first foreclosure, filed bankruptcy, and moved back in with my mother, all just before giving birth to my second child.

What I didn't understand then, but absolutely see now, is that **my money habits were trauma responses.**

I wasn't just shopping; I was **soothing**.

I wasn't just overextending.

I was **overcompensating** . . . for years of feeling not good enough, not worthy enough, not *together* enough.

The ghost of not being "materially enough" haunted me from the fitting room to the closing table. I believed that if I could just do all the outward things that people who had "enough money" did, I could finally *feel* like I was enough.

Spoiler alert: That's not how it works.

From ages thirteen to thirty-five, I kept myself in financial bondage as I tried to outrun emotional wounds with receipts and transactions. I wasn't budgeting; I was bandaging.

One of my mentors used to say, *"Money ain't the most important thing, but it's right up there with oxygen."*

He wasn't wrong.

Money is required to live, and even more is required to raise children, dream big, and navigate the world with choices. **But what I lacked wasn't just money.** I lacked the *internal foundation* to manage it.

I had expensive dreams, a strong work ethic, zero financial knowledge, a fractured self-image, and no emotional space to realize I was missing every crucial ingredient.

I was not going to outrun my brokenness.

I was a walking contradiction: all potential, no peace.

All productivity, no pause.

A whirlwind of aspiration layered over confusion.

Imagine the ripples . . .

The impact wasn't just on my bank account.

The ripples touched my children, my relationships, my self-worth, and my ability to trust myself with abundance.

Pause & Reflect

When the Numbers Tell a Deeper Story

We like to think of money as math. Numbers. Logic.

But for many of us, especially those shaped by trauma, money is *emotion*.

It's identity.

It's a way to soothe or prove or disappear.

And what I learned, the hard way, is that unhealed chaos doesn't stay contained.

Here's what I still reflect on:

- **Chaos in my spirit led to chaos in my finances.**

  I didn't feel worthy. I didn't feel seen. I didn't feel *safe*.

  So I spent to feel powerful.

  I spent to feel put-together.

  I spent to avoid feeling anything at all.

  What have you bought, not because you needed it, but because you needed to feel like ***you*** *were enough?*

- **Chaos in my finances bled into every other part of life.**

  It wasn't just overdrafts or repossessions.

  It was shame. Stress. Strain in my relationships. Emotional exhaustion.

  Because when the bottom falls out financially, the weight isn't just on your bank account. It presses down on your entire sense of self.

Where has financial stress stolen your energy, your joy, or your voice?

- **It was all circular dysfunction.**

The inner pain led to the bad decisions.

The bad decisions created more pain.

I kept chasing stability but running in emotional circles.

And the only thing that could stop it? . . . **A violent interruption of the pattern.**

The point isn't shame.

The point is awareness.

Because once you see the pattern, you can begin to break it.

IV

MAMA, I MADE IT! (ON ACCIDENT)

Time doesn't stop for anyone, and neither did I.

After the heartbreak of my first love, I kept moving. Not because I'd healed, but because motion was the only language I knew. I didn't have the tools to process grief or name trauma—I only knew how to outrun it.

So I went looking for what I thought would make it stop hurting.

Love. Or something like it.

That ache, left by abandonment, unworthiness, and the aftershocks of trauma, pushed me into overdrive. Somewhere along the way, I met the man who would become my first husband. Compared to what I'd known, he felt . . . safe. He was nice. Predictable. Seemed to want me.

At the time, I mistook consistency for care. Security for love.

So I said yes. To him. To building a life. To burying my pain in structure, stability, and striving.

But underneath it all, I was still chasing something. Not a man. Not a marriage. But *enoughness.*

My mother used to say, *"Nicole, if you get a master's degree, you'll be able to write your own check."*

And I was a good kid. So I did what my mama said.

I graduated in the top 10 percent of my high school class. Earned a full ride to one of the state universities. Finished my bachelor's degree at twenty-four, my master's at twenty-seven. All while getting married, giving birth to three children, and buying two homes and three cars, between the ages of twenty-one and twenty-six.

I was productive. Accomplished.

But I was also deeply unwell.

Wounded. Disconnected. Performing wellness while barely hanging on.

My coping mechanism had become performance.

I was addicted to doing because stillness meant feeling.

And feeling terrified me.

Behind the smiling pictures and milestone celebrations was a woman silencing herself.

A woman managing unaddressed rape, internalized self-hatred, and generational expectations, all under the disguise of "progress."

Suppression might be the best word here.

Anyway . . .

I was in the middle of my MBA program and had just given birth to my youngest son when the familiar restlessness crept in again. I was starting to feel boxed in at work. I knew the place wasn't valuing me the way it should. But as usual, I stayed longer than I should have.

Eventually, I started looking for my next move.

Updated the résumé. Hit the job boards.

And then, an email. A well-known company was interested. I vaguely remembered the name from my undergrad classes but hadn't connected the dots. Even after some basic research, I still didn't fully grasp the level of prestige.

Then the offer came. A 50 percent salary increase.

Holy shit, I thought. At twenty-six, I was making nearly the same salary as my mother.

I guess that master's degree was writing the check after all.

But what I didn't realize was how unequipped I truly was.

The company was elite. Demanding. Razor sharp. It refined me in the best ways . . . and shattered me in the worst.

Because even in that high-rise office, with a polished résumé and a corner on "success," I still felt like I didn't belong.

The ghost that followed me into that role wasn't imposter syndrome.

It was *unworthiness.*

And the illusion?

That I could finally outrun it if I just achieved enough. Proved enough. Produced enough.

Pause & Reflect

When the Room Revealed the Mirror

I used to think this job broke me.

The pressure. The pace. The politics.

But the truth?

It didn't break me. It *exposed* me.

Not because I wasn't capable.

But because I never believed I was *enough* to begin with.

Here's what I still reflect on:

- **I never thought I was enough; this environment just revealed it to me.**

  I didn't walk in with confidence. I walked in with performance. I overcompensated before anyone even asked me to, because in my head, I was already playing catch-up.

  What spaces have revealed your insecurities instead of causing them?

- **I was prejudiced; I valued my experiences less simply because I was Black and walking into a professional environment that was never designed for me to succeed.**

  My own internal bias made me assume my background was inferior, even when my results spoke otherwise.

Whose table did you try to shrink yourself to fit at . . . not realizing you brought the feast?

- **This was when my self-sacrifice multiplied.**

I gave more. Stayed later. Bit my tongue. Proved. Performed. Persisted. All in the name of being worthy of the seat I'd already earned.

What did you give away in the name of proving yourself?

Ironically, this was only a prelude of things to come in my life. I could no longer cover my breaking points with my accomplishments.

V

FALSE FLAGGING SUCCESS . . . I GOT THE "BIG JOB"

Getting a job at a large organization felt like something straight out of a '70s sitcom, a scene where the Black daughter of a hard-working single mom breaks through every barrier and lands a "big job." That's exactly how it felt in my family. Both surprising and expected. Like all the work I'd put in had finally *done something*. We didn't know what the payoff would look like. We just knew there had to be one.

What most folks didn't know was that I'd been working my whole life. At ten, I was roller-skating groceries to customers' cars for tips at the local store. By thirteen, I had my first W2 job through a state-funded program for low-income families.

At sixteen, I was balancing full-time high school with as many restaurant shifts as I could grab. Work ethic wasn't something I developed; it was something I'd always had. It was my survival strategy.

So by the time I walked through the doors of that organization, I brought both power and baggage with me. I believed I was smart, driven, resourceful, and I was. But I also believed I could only go so far. Somewhere deep down, I'd accepted that Black people, especially ones like me, didn't climb *all* the way. We just made it "far enough."

And in that environment, I was probably one of the sharpest people in every room, but also the most self-doubting. I didn't know it yet, but I was teaching others how to treat me . . . because I didn't fully believe I belonged.

Four months into the role, my phone rang. My father was in the hospital. Stage 4 stomach cancer that had already begun its silent invasion of his body, likely spreading to his colon by then.

It was a gut-punch, and not just because of the diagnosis.

It was the full collision of who he'd been . . . and who I thought I had to be now.

Let me explain.

My father was a crack addict and had been for most of my life. One of my earliest memories of him was him stealing my Christmas present to support his addiction. Still, he was my father. And when I got that call, I went. Immediately.

When I walked into his hospital room, he and the nurses shared the news—terminal. No real treatment options. Just pain management and end-of-life planning. There was talk of state-funded hospice care, public aid nursing homes.

And somewhere between the awkward hospital lighting and the quiet defeat in his eyes, I said, "You know I got that *big job*, Daddy."

I meant it as comfort. As code for, *We'll be okay. I'll figure something out.*

It was my way of saying I could carry it. That I *had* to.

But here's the truth I didn't realize until years later:

That "big job" was a lower-level professional role. Bottom of the totem pole. Not a leadership track. Not a seat at the table.

But in my world? That job was a *dream*. Because I didn't know how much more was actually possible. Not for people like me. Not for Black girls from the Englewood neighborhood in Chicago.

That moment, calling it a "big job" was my first conscious encounter with the truth of my own limiting beliefs.

That's why the memory still stings. Not because I "lied" to him. But because I believed what I was saying without understanding the limit in it.

That experience would sharpen me in ways no classroom ever could. It would expose me to global excellence, demand my very best, and still teach me, over and over again, that my best wasn't enough. Not *there*. Not *like this*.

The ghost I was fighting in that space wasn't my father's absence, or even the grief I carried for him as he declined. The ghost was *me*, or at least the version of me that thought she had to perform her way into being enough.

What I didn't know then is that this job, this role I once saw as the finish line, would become the *starting line* of a different kind of journey. A journey of self-validation. Of unlearning. Of seeing myself, not through the eyes of my family or my employer, but through my own healed lens.

Pause & Reflect

Sometimes the Breakthrough Is Also a Reflection

That "big job" felt like proof that all the struggle had meant something. That the hustle, the sacrifice, and the survival finally added up.

But underneath that pride was a quieter truth: I'd been carrying everyone's expectations, including my own.

In that moment, I wasn't just showing up for opportunity—I was showing up for legacy. For the little girl who hustled tips on roller skates. For the daughter trying to rewrite her father's ending.

For the family who needed someone to "make it."

Here's what I still reflect on:

- **In coming to my father's side, I was jumping an ocean for someone who never walked over a puddle for me.**

  I'd been molded that reciprocal care and concern were for other people. Not me.

  Where in your life have you overextended yourself to earn love, approval, or redemption that was never yours to carry?

- **I placed myself in the role of my family's answer.**

  It was never mine to carry, yet it was so natural and expensive (in many ways) for me to do.

  Where have you placed an expectation of yourself blindly? What did it cost? What would it feel like to give it back?

- **That job set me on the path that I'm on today . . .**

  Something that could seem so small in today's reflection is one of the catalysts for the book you're reading right now. Maybe it was the "big job."

  What "small" moments in your life could be shaping your biggest transformation?

Every "big job," every painful reckoning, every mirror moment is preparing you for the version of yourself who no longer performs—but simply **IS**.

VI

"DEMON SEED"

"White woman tears."

A loaded phrase. A cultural critique.

An American colloquialism used to describe how White women, intentionally or not, can weaponize perceived fragility in ways that protect themselves while punishing others, especially Black women.

It's a phrase that makes people uncomfortable.

It should.

Because it reflects a pattern that's both subtle and insidious, where some people's pain gets protected, while others are expected to swallow theirs and keep performing.

When I started at the firm, I believed excellence would be my equalizer.

I wasn't just a high performer; I was elite.

In less than a year, I earned my first promotion. I was overseeing the largest and most complex portfolio in our region.

My forecasting was on point. My team's numbers always hit. I consistently outperformed my peers, delivering results with a third less time and support.

And I did it while managing a full home life—three children, a marriage, a mortgage, and a master's degree in progress.

I believed all the right things:

That 95 percent of success was just showing up.

That merit spoke louder than politics.

That I could outwork bias.

So when my mother voiced concerns about how Black women were treated in white spaces, I smiled politely. But inside, I brushed it off.

I thought her fears were from another era.

I was succeeding.

I was being rewarded.

Until I wasn't.

The 2008 crash hit, and everything shifted.

Budgets tightened. Teams reorganized. Behaviors changed.

That's when she came, an older White woman transferred from another department.

On paper, she had more years of experience. However, in my practical experience, I found her forecasts were often outside of target. My assessment of her skills was that she seemed to lack the strategic clarity I'd been praised for.

But somehow, she was quickly favored.

Where I was "sharp," she was "sweet."

Where I was "prepared," she was "trying."

Where I was "direct," she was "emotional."

And when her results were openly in question?

She cried.

She played overwhelmed.

And the room wrapped its arms around her.

Meanwhile, I—the team lead—was left managing not just the workload but her passive resistance. Requests sometimes went unanswered . . . key deadlines overlooked. And, at times, she was outwardly rude.

I finally brought my concerns to our shared manager.

And instead of support, I got reprimanded.

I was told she was "going through a lot."

That I needed to be more sensitive.

That I needed to be more of a team player.

Her White fragility was protected.

My Black excellence was interrogated.

That moment didn't just sting professionally; it was another emotional prick.

This workplace didn't just challenge my competence. It amplified every trauma I hadn't healed.

I'd spent years proving I could rise above abandonment, rape, self-doubt, and shame.

I buried pain in productivity.

I wore performance like armor.

But no armor could shield me from a culture that refused to see me.

Where my results didn't matter.

Where my truth was too strong.

Where my silence was the only thing that felt safe.

I went on leave not long after. I was emotionally, physically, spiritually spent.

Three weeks into my leave, she quit.

Turns out, she couldn't do the job without me after all.

Pause & Reflect

When "Demon Seed" Wasn't the Real Problem

In therapy, and at home, my nickname for her became "Demon Seed."

Dramatic? Maybe.

But when you're being slowly crushed under the weight of someone else's protected mediocrity . . . the name fit.

Her gaslighting, her passive defiance, her tears—all of it spun me into emotional chaos.

But over time, the truth got clearer:

"Demon Seed" was never the real enemy.

She was just the trigger.

I was the one already carrying the wounds.

Here's what I've since unpacked:

- **"Demon Seed" was the name I gave this woman in my therapy and at-home venting sessions. I should never have let her enter my psyche this way.**

  She didn't earn that much rent-free space in my mind.

  What names, or narratives, have you given power to—that now need to be evicted?

- **I, not "Demon Seed," was the root of my issues.**

  She didn't create my doubt. She just awakened the ghosts already living in me: the unworthiness, the need to prove, the trauma I'd buried under success.

What situations have exposed your unhealed places, not by breaking you, but by revealing you?

- **Hmmm . . . maybe this was the "big job"?!**

Not because of the paycheck. Not even the prestige.

But because it forced a confrontation with my deepest wounds.

It was the mirror. The training ground. It led to the necessary unraveling.

Have you ever been blessed with a breaking that became your breakthrough?

This was the setup.
The moment before the shift.
The last inhale before the violent interruption.

It was coming.
And it wasn't going to be quiet.

VII

THEY TOOK THEIR TOYS (PROJECTS) AWAY . . . AND MY VALIDATION WITH IT

They don't actually teach Gaslighting 101 in corporate leadership, but they might as well. It's an unspoken core curriculum in places where accountability is inconvenient and power protects itself. I got my first real baptism in it at this employer.

Looking back, I now see how perfectly primed I was for the lesson.

One of the most consistent themes of my life, from childhood through young adulthood, was that I was a *"good girl."* I followed the rules. I trusted authority. I believed that if I worked hard, stayed honest, and didn't make too much noise, I'd be rewarded, seen, and ultimately valued.

It wasn't just a personality trait; it was conditioning.

Growing up, my mom bragged on me every chance she got. I'd curl up under her like a content kitten, purring from the warmth of her praise. Teachers reinforced it too. I lived for report card days. The gold stars. The glowing comments. I was trained to equate approval with goodness, and goodness with worth.

So when I entered the workplace, I showed up with that same eager spirit. I trusted the process. I believed results would speak for themselves. I kept delivering because that had always been the formula. And for a while, it worked. Promotions. Recognition. Extra bonuses. Special projects. I was doing the "right" things, and the system rewarded me. That was the deal. Or so I thought.

Then 2008 hit—and the rules changed.

The global financial crash brought more than an economic downturn. It also exposed the fragility of workplace "meritocracies." Suddenly, the behaviors and outcomes that once earned me praise started getting picked apart. I was no longer celebrated; I was scrutinized.

Tone. Word choice. Visibility. I was told there weren't many special projects available, and even if there were, I didn't sit on the "right floor" to be seen. I asked to move floors and was told there was no space.

WTF?!

Meanwhile, people from that very floor kept coming to me, asking for help with their work.

And I gave it.

Because I was still playing by the old rules. I believed we were collaborating. I believed we were being "team players." I believed that if I shared my tools, like the budget forecasting model I had built, they'd appreciate me for it.

Instead, one colleague took that tool straight to leadership, passed it off as her own, got rewarded with a new project . . . and later, a promotion.

The worst part? I congratulated her on the elevator, not yet understanding what had happened. She smiled and told me the leadership team had been so impressed. And I stood there, gut sinking, smile fixed, realizing that I'd been played.

DOUBLE WTF

When I raised concerns about fairness and integrity, I became the problem. The feedback I received became less about the quality of my work and more about how I made others feel. About tone. About perception. About being "difficult."

It wasn't about the substance. It was about control.

I was being managed, not developed.

I didn't realize it at the time, but the organization had stopped evaluating my contributions and started managing my presence. The more I asked questions, the more isolated I became. My confidence, once rooted in outcomes, began to shrink under the weight of whispered criticisms and shifting expectations.

And it crushed me.

Because I'd unknowingly placed the keys to my self-worth in their hands. When they decided I no longer fit the narrative, they quietly changed the locks. And I was left outside, wondering what I'd done wrong.

This was how the system gaslit me.

It didn't tell me I was crazy; it just slowly made me question my value. And I believed it. Because I'd been trained to.

I used to think the devastation came from the betrayal.

But what really broke me was realizing I had never questioned the rules I'd built my life around.

They weren't written for me.

And yet, I followed them anyway. Because good girls always do.

Until we don't.

Pause & Reflect

When Good Girl Training Becomes a Setup

I thought I was just being responsible. Respectful. Driven.

But what I was really being . . .

Was *conditioned.*

Trained from the sandbox to the staff meeting to let other people tell me who I was, and who I wasn't.

- **I'd been trained from childhood to let other people tell me who I was.**

  The gold stars. The good grades. The glowing praise.

  They taught me to look outward for validation before I ever knew how to look inward for truth.

  Who taught you to believe that approval equals identity?

- **Damn, I was a gullible adult.**

  I didn't just drink the Kool-Aid, I poured the cups and passed them out.

  I believed in the process. In the idea of fairness. In the system.

  Even as it unraveled in front of me, I kept trying to follow the old rules.

  What did it take for you to finally stop playing by rules that were never designed for your victory?

This was an absolute turning point.

I didn't know it yet, but the disillusionment was the invitation.

The breakdown was the doorway.

This was the moment I stopped being the "good girl" and started becoming the grown woman.

What moment in your story was painful, but necessary? The crack that let the truth in?

VIII

SPEAKING OF GASLIGHTING (BACK TO THIS MARRIAGE THING)

By the second year of our marriage, I knew it wasn't going to work. I remember the exact moment the realization hit me, and, just as quickly, I buried it. I'd been trained since childhood to distrust my own instincts, to silence the internal alarms.

Pain had taught me how to override truth. And truth be told, I didn't want to believe it. I was still the over-functioning, over-performing, overcompensating little girl trying to turn dysfunction into something redeemable.

Looking back, the signs were glaring. We were on the same road but moving in different directions, and I'd convinced myself that our proximity meant partnership. I'd always been the idealistic realist, dreaming, but with a plan. I set goals, and I executed. I fought hard. I achieved harder. I made things happen.

He also dreamed. But that's where it stopped. He was charismatic, thoughtful on the surface, and full of potential. But potential without work is just performance, and he was far better at performing than progressing. He liked the idea of success, but not the discomfort required to achieve it.

His passivity masked something deeper. He often dodged accountability, distorted conversations, and weaponized my standards as the problem. My attempts to raise concerns seemed to be twisted into questions that made me doubt myself. My voice had always been the one most dismissed, even by me. And in this marriage, that pattern carried through.

The 2008 crash only magnified what was already crumbling. His layoff became the official turning point. Our agreement was that he would use the time to start a business while caring for the kids. It seemed fair. I was stretched thin at work, grinding through the pressure of corporate politics and chasing the illusion of upward mobility. The idea was that he'd take the entrepreneurial lead so that eventually I could step away too.

Instead, most days, I came home to chaos: a messy house, incomplete projects, and kids who were learning half-measured habits while he played the role of the more lighthearted parent. He rarely finished anything he started. Routine household maintenance was mostly ignored. Follow-through on school support meetings and even haircuts for our sons was often left to me—despite cutting his own hair since his teenage years. He let the house fall apart, just like he let our vision of life fall apart.

Worse still, he began to manipulate our daughter's perception of me, presenting himself as her "safe space" while painting me as harsh or unavailable. In truth, I was buried. Exhausted. Carrying the load of five people with the capacity of one soul.

And yet, I kept showing up. Just like I always had.

Just like I did in childhood, when I took care of my emotional world in silence, when I internalized everyone else's pain as my responsibility, when I learned to equate love with survival.

I told myself that staying was noble. That I was protecting the kids. That maybe love really did require sacrifice, especially from the one who could handle it.

But here's the reality: I wasn't handling it.

I'd gained eighty pounds. I was isolated. I was numb. I looked in the mirror and barely recognized myself. My body had become the only thing I could control, and even that was slipping through my fingers. But the deepest fracture wasn't in my weight or my marriage; it was in my belief that this was all somehow my fault.

That lie? It didn't start with him.

It started long before, when I was a child taught to normalize harm, to mistrust myself, to believe that enduring was the same thing as being strong.

The same thing I did with Matt in the bathroom. It was the same story, just with a different villain.

Pause & Reflect

When Denial Wore a Wedding Ring

I didn't want to believe it was failing.

So I *made it work.*

I adjusted. I explained. I compensated.

And then I called it love.

But denial is tricky like that, especially when you're trying to protect the picture you painted for your life.

Here's what I had to face:

- **I was in denial about who he was versus who he pretended to be.**

  He sold me charm, warmth, and vision. I bought the whole package and ignored the receipts.

  What truths have you excused because the story felt better than the facts?

- **I kept myself in denial by consistently making up for his shortcomings and giving "us" the credit.**

  My effort. My overtime. My sacrifices. All stamped with a shared signature **we** didn't earn.

  Where have you confused your solo effort for partnership?

- **I tricked myself into believing that staying was better for the kids.**

  But what they saw wasn't stability; it was sacrifice. A mother unraveling while trying to hold up a house of cards.

  What have you called "protection" that was actually self-betrayal?

This wasn't just a slow erosion.

It was the final stretch before the earthquake.

IX

FUCK THIS SHIT—I'M OUT (THE TWO-STEP TO FREEDOM)

I believe God gave me a few superpowers: resilience, endurance, and a still, small voice (as the old folks used to say) that refuses to let me die in places I don't belong.

For most of my life, I didn't know how to listen to that voice early. I'd drown it in "shoulds" and guilt and the performance of holding it all together. But eventually, when things around me got too out of alignment with my truth, that voice would rise. And I'd move.

Around year ten of my marriage, right as my job was starting to unravel, I started going to therapy. Not because I thought I deserved healing, but because I thought I was doing something wrong.

I was exhausted. Mentally. Emotionally. Spiritually. I doubted myself . . . and the internal conversations I was having? Brutal.

I started therapy through the EAP benefits at work. I didn't even know what I was looking for, just that I couldn't keep feeling the way I felt.

And then I found her.

A wise, older Black woman who took one look at me and saw past the job title, the degrees, the marriage, the smile. I looked like a mess and didn't even know it. I'd gained weight. My light was dim. But I thought I was "fine" because I was still high-achieving.

About a year into treatment, she told me, "You look like a different woman than the one who first walked through that door." And she was right.

In those early sessions, she was the first person who helped me name what was happening, not just at work, but at home.

She told me my husband's behavior was passive-aggressive. "They call it crazy-making behavior," she said. "Because it makes *you* feel like you're losing your mind."

My experience was that every time we made a goal as a couple, the pattern repeated:

- He'd act excited and talk a good game.
- He'd dabble in the work until it got hard.
- Then he'd start poking holes in the plan.
- Then he'd quit.
- Then he'd find a way to blame me for the fallout.
- Then he'd retreat to "find his peace."

Rinse. Repeat. Over. And over.

If I called him out, it was, *"You're too controlling,"* or *"You're overthinking it,"* or *"It doesn't take all that."*

And because I'd spent a lifetime overriding my own instincts, I believed him. I second-guessed myself. I still wanted to be the "good girl" who didn't disappoint people.

But one night, I went home and looked up the definition of passive-aggressive.

And I finally saw it in black and white:

It was how I was experiencing him.

And I was the one making myself crazy trying to compensate.

That realization—that I wasn't crazy, just being driven there—ignited that voice in me.

It took years to fully break free. But I did.

I left the job in 2011. I left the marriage in 2017.

Not because I had a plan. Not because the timing was perfect.

But because the voice inside me *finally screamed loud enough* and I had no choice but to move.

This wasn't some pretty breakthrough moment.

This was a *violent interruption* in the patterns of treatment I was trained to allow.

At this time, I just "couldn't" do it anymore. In the near future, I would change my language from "can't" to "won't" . . . and we'll get to that later.

It was the season that I stopped explaining and *started exiting.*

I bet on me.

And it was the best damn decision I've ever made.

Pause & Reflect

When Survival Becomes Self-Betrayal

There's a difference between enduring and living.

Between holding it together and being held together.

I didn't know the difference—until the mirror cracked.

Here's what I had to learn in the "fire":

- **When you can't see yourself clearly, look at what you've completed.**

  I was lost in confusion about who I was . . . but the evidence of my resilience was everywhere.

  What have you survived that you've never fully given yourself credit for?

- **Be honest with yourself about what is and what is not working.**

  I kept telling myself "it's not that bad" just to keep functioning.

  What truths are you avoiding because you're scared of what they'll cost?

- **Courage is easier to muster when you hate all your options.**

  I didn't leave because I had it all figured out. I left because staying was killing me quietly.

What would you finally walk away from if comfort wasn't your currency?

This was the interruption.
Not the one I wanted.
But the one I couldn't ***live*** without.

FINDING THE LOVE

Journaling has always been a sanity saver for me. It would be no different in this period of my life. For each era of my life, my journal signatures were thematic. The signature theme for this period was "Finding the Love" because I felt so unloved and neglected by the majority of the people around me.

What I'm confident that I'll discover if/when I ever go back to read those entries is that the person I was most disconnected from was me. I didn't know my own voice. I didn't trust myself. I couldn't hear my own heart.

This void left me in constant need of external confirmation and validation, which also kept me at constant risk of being exploited.

Love is a verb. Demonstrating love to myself was going to take courageous action. I was going to have to face myself and start intentionally dealing with all the things that made me feel smothered.

"Finding the Love" started with listening to my own voice. ***Keeping the love*** is a daily focus of honoring that very voice.

I

PAY ATTENTION TO THE SIGNS

I was at the heaviest weight I'd ever been, physically, emotionally, and spiritually. We were in year six of negotiating through the foreclosure on the home we'd lived in for a decade. My then-husband was, once again, out of work, and the full weight of the family's survival fell on me. I was holding it all together for everyone else while crumbling quietly under the weight of it all.

Every day, I felt myself dying a little more. That's not dramatic; it's simply true. The longer I allowed this man to drain me emotionally, psychologically, and financially, the more of myself I lost.

He'd become a vulture, perched and patient, feeding off of my ambition, my stability, and my capacity.

For years, he used the goals we once made together as weapons, flipping my drive into accusations of "doing too much" and making it seem as if our family was a casualty of my belief in excellence. In our home and to the world (those who didn't know us), he wore the mask of a strong provider. The truth is, I carried the vast majority of our familial responsibilities behind closed doors.

SIGN NO. 1: MOTHER'S DAY, 2017

We were at a family breakfast. Like most occasions, I was the one who made the plans, got everyone out the door, and paid the bill, even on *Mother's Day*. I smiled like I always did, a reflex now more than a feeling, while something inside me lost a little more respect.

In an effort to be lighthearted, my daughter showed me a clip from one of their favorite cartoons. In it, a mom comes home from work to a wrecked house. Her husband and three kids had done nothing all day. With one snap of her finger, everything stopped; the entire neighborhood shook. She grabbed them by the neck (husband included) and, in a demonic voice, demanded they clean up the mess.

It was meant to be funny. And it was. Until it wasn't.

As we left the restaurant, still laughing, my daughter nudged me and said: "Her name is Nicole . . . just like you. And she also has three kids and a fat, lazy husband."

I froze. Laughed a little. Swallowed hard.

What. The. Hell?! . . . What was I actually modeling for my children?

I'd already been feeling the ground shift under me, wondering whether I was clinging to a marriage out of fear or familiarity.

But that moment? That was the last spark. A reflection I hadn't asked for, but couldn't unsee.

If this was marriage, if *this* was what I'd been fighting to preserve, then marriage wasn't for me.

SIGN NO. 2

That question—*"What am I really showing my kids?"*—haunted me.

Within days, I was researching divorce attorneys. I still struggled with my Hero Syndrome. I worried more about how my leaving would impact him than how staying was destroying me. I even prayed, not for strength to go, but for him to be *okay* after I left. I wanted to believe that somehow, he'd land safely, and that would give me permission to walk away.

And then, I had a wild, random thought: *Wouldn't it be something if his sister needed a place to stay?* She'd gone back and forth a few times. They could help each other. He wouldn't be alone. I wouldn't feel guilty.

I laughed it off . . . but tucked it into the back of my mind.

Then, literally the day before my attorney appointment, he got a call.

His sister needed a place to stay. Again.

I stood there stunned. A little amused. A little terrified.

Really, God?

That Monday morning, I negotiated with him to keep the shared car. A few hours later, I walked out of my attorney's office having signed the papers and written the $600 retainer check.

No more signs. No more waiting. No more saving anyone but me.

Pause & Reflect

When the Mirror Comes from a Child

It wasn't just a cartoon.

It wasn't just a joke.

It was the truth, reflected back at me from the mouth of my own daughter.

I'd been holding everything together while he coasted on appearances.

Propping up a man who didn't pull his weight.

Funding the lifestyle, managing the emotions, making the home, keeping the "peace."

And I was doing it at the cost of myself.

Here's what I now understand:

- **I was enabling him to destroy me while I was propping up his fake image.**

  I called it "keeping the family stable." But what I was really doing was handing over the tools he used to chip away at me.

  What do you call survival that slowly kills you?

- **The kids always see the real truth.**

  Even when they can't name it. Even when we're trying to shield them. They see who shows up and who hides. Who sacrifices and who avoids.

  What have your children been witnessing while you've been trying to protect them?

- **Lean into the signs when you've asked for them.**

  I prayed for clarity. I *got* clarity. The question wasn't whether I had divine permission to go. The question was whether I was brave enough to listen.

  What signs have you received that you've been too scared to act on?

This was no longer about keeping a marriage.

It was about reclaiming a life.

And that began with choosing myself. Loudly, clearly, and unapologetically.

11

CHANGING PLACES: PLUCKING MYSELF OUT OF THE TOXICITY

The first of many necessities on the road to *Finding the Love* was physically changing my surroundings.

I've always believed that your environment either reflects what's going on inside or directly impacts it. For too many years, I'd been living in a space that mirrored my exhaustion, my grief, and the slow erosion of my spirit.

The house was neglected, inside and out. The lawn overgrown, the paint chipped, the rooms cluttered and dim. It looked like how I felt.

It was the middle of June when I told him I was done. No blow-up. No big scene. Just a quiet decision followed by movement. His sister and her family had recently moved in, and I, like always, was already preparing for my next pivot.

But as my decision took root, the mind games crept in.

He started telling me I couldn't afford to leave.

Looking back, that's *laughable*. But in the moment? I believed it . . . just for a little while. I was conditioned to doubt myself.

What I eventually realized was that I *couldn't* afford to keep supporting *him*.

What was actually being communicated was that I couldn't afford to leave *him* comfortable. Gaslighting, once again, disguised as logic.

This time, though? I was listening to myself.

And I was dreaming, actively, for the first time in years.

I dreamed of a space where my spirit could breathe. Where I could walk barefoot on clean floors, sip tea in sunlight, decorate with color and softness, and wake up in a space that reflected *me*. I craved peace. Order. Wholeness. And maybe even a little bit of joy.

So I started small: a solar-powered dancing toy, a glass teapot, fresh flowers, a five-pound gummy bear. (Yes, random—but joyful.) Each item was a reclaiming. A reminder. A step back toward myself.

We agreed to stay in the same neighborhood for the kids. I assumed I'd be renting an apartment. I told myself I couldn't afford more. My credit was still wrecked, and honestly, my confidence was fragile too. But I kept searching, just in case.

Then I saw it.

A home listed just above apartment rent. Modest. Quirky. Full of sunlight. I pulled up, parked in the back, and *felt it* immediately: *This is it.*

The moment I walked in, the brightness of the home hit me like a memory. It reminded me of my grandmother—of her sunlit living room, her open windows, the warmth she brought into every space she touched. That brightness lived here too. It felt sacred. Familiar. *Mine.*

I told the owners my story. Honestly. I acknowledged my credit situation and offered a plan: If they allowed me to paint and prepare the home over the next two months, I'd pay in installments until the full deposit and first month's rent were met. I gave my word, and I kept it.

They agreed to take a chance on me.

I moved in on January 13, 2018, with a few belongings, a list of dreams, and a deep desire to fill that home with things that reflected *who I really was*. It wasn't just a move. It was a homecoming.

To myself.

Pause & Reflect

When the House Reflected My Heart

It wasn't just about moving.

It wasn't just about furniture or rent.

It was about choosing a space that finally looked like *me*, not the mess I'd been surviving.

For the first time in years, my environment didn't drain me.

It energized me.

It mirrored the woman I was unearthing as I was stripping off everyone else's labels.

Here's what I learned in the process:

- **Do the things that make your spirit smile and your heart happy.**

  Joy doesn't have to be big or expensive. A teapot. A dancing toy. A sunlit room. Those weren't just objects; they were reminders that I was worth delight.

  What simple joys have you been depriving yourself of?

- **Make a strategic plan and execute accordingly.**

  Leaving wasn't impulsive; it was intentional. I mapped it. Budgeted it. Negotiated it.

  Healing doesn't mean you stop being practical. It means your planning finally includes *you*.

  What would shift if you built a strategy around your freedom, not just your survival?

- **Being vulnerable is worth the risk in the right situation.**

  Telling the truth about my credit. Asking for a chance. Trusting someone to see past my scars. Vulnerability got me the keys to my new home, and to a new chapter.

  Where are you being called to take a risk on being real?

This wasn't just a new home. It was a fresh start in every sense of those words.

It was about building a life that felt like love (like me), on purpose.

And it started with a door I was brave enough to open.

III

THE RECOVERY: GIVING MYSELF TIME AND SPACE

The comforts of my new space were more than visual. They were metaphysical.

It was clean. Cozy. Quiet.

Heavy on the sunshine, light on the emotional weight.

For the first time in years, there was no in-house toxicity. Just peace.

I savored the simplest things: a consistently clean bathroom. Matching towel sets. A cushy rug under my feet. I splurged on a quality bedroom set and a mattress that cradled my body like it had waited for me to come home to myself. I brought in plants and candy jars—tiny echoes of my grandmother's spirit. I placed those jars in different corners of the house so that anyone who visited could experience an unexpected moment of joy, the same way she had once done for me.

I bought a high-end soundbar so I could fill the air with soul-healing music. Loud and often.

I started buying fresh food. Cooking became a ritual. It was creative, nourishing, sacred.

Our custody schedule alternated weeks. During my weeks with the kids, my energy was laser-focused on them. I made sure they were caught up in school, something their father rarely paid attention to. I got them into activities, into a rhythm, a structure, and I tried to give them my version of joy. I wanted them to feel the kind of home and intentionality I'd always wanted for myself.

And when they weren't with me? I gave that same energy to *me*.

Sure, I was still doing things for others, because that's who I am. But I only did what I *wanted* to do. For the first time in my adult life, no one's needs came before my own. And that shift changed everything.

My journaling deepened . . . and so did my awareness.

As I wrote, I started to notice that outside voices were very present on my pages. Thoughts shaped by guilt, fear, and expectations that weren't mine would show up dressed as my own. I had to catch myself.

I'd stop. Reread. And then rewrite.

Not until the words resonated in my spirit did I move on. It was an active process of peeling back the layers and learning to recognize my voice. Not the one conditioned to not like myself. Not the compromised one. *Mine.*

I was shedding weight in every sense of the word.

Within six months, I'd dropped almost fifty pounds, effortlessly. It wasn't some new plan or fitness craze. It was the natural byproduct of peace.

I was no longer stuffing pain or feeding a life that didn't nourish me in return.

One day, while traveling for work, I passed a full-length mirror in my hotel room. I stopped. Then stared.

Not because I saw something unfamiliar.

But because for the first time in years, I *recognized* the woman looking back at me.

She wasn't weighed down.

She wasn't hiding behind exhaustion or shame.

She wasn't trying to smile through heartbreak.

She was grounded. Hopeful. Clear-eyed.

And damn, she was beautiful.

Not the performative kind of beautiful that needs permission or praise.

But the kind rooted in self-definition.

The kind of beauty that comes from alignment as opposed to approval.

This was the woman I had always imagined.

And now she was here. In full form.

And *she* was not up for negotiation.

I was finally seeing the real me.

And I wasn't going back.

Pause & Reflect

When the Mirror Tells the Truth

It wasn't about the towels.

Or the rugs. Or the plants. Or even the candy jars.

It was about *me*. I finally created a world that felt like mine.

One where peace wasn't earned through performance.

One where joy didn't come second to survival.

One where I could hear myself, see myself, *be* myself.

For the first time in a long time, my reflection wasn't asking for permission.

It was offering proof.

Here's what I now understand:

- **This marked the beginning of stripping off those labels.**

  The ones others gave me. The ones I wore to stay safe. The ones I carried so long I forgot they weren't mine.

  What labels have you outgrown that you're still trying to squeeze into?

- **I never would have gotten here if I hadn't started to trust myself.**

  Not the loud, performative voice. The quiet one. The one whispering, *"This way, love. You already know."*

  What parts of yourself have been trying to guide you, even while you ignored them?

- **Finding my authentic self is the highest prized gift I've ever given myself.**

It didn't come wrapped in ease. It came through fire. Through clarity. Through intentional choice.

What would it look like to stop abandoning yourself, and to start honoring who you've always been?

In the new home I'd found space and a foundation . . .

This was the foundation for the *real* home.
The one I was building inside me.

IV

BITTER MAN CHRONICLES

It's often said that "hell hath no fury like a woman scorned." I'd argue that "the fury of a bitter ex-husband will give both hell and a scorned woman a run for their money."

I was completely unprepared for how bitter my ex-husband would become after I left. And even more unprepared for the levels he would stoop to.

People who had known us for years were shocked that I didn't see it coming. Their responses were some version of: "But he's always been that way. You just didn't acknowledge it."

Then came the part about how much I loved him. How I was so committed to keeping the family together that I refused to see what was obvious.

They were right.

And my inner committee never missed the chance to chime in with a sarcastic, "You big dummy," in the voice of my favorite childhood sitcom character.

For the last few years of our marriage, we rarely had sex.

He slept on the couch more nights than not, and I was relieved. I thought it was because he was inconsiderate, up late playing video games, and disruptive to my sleep. But looking back, it wasn't just laziness or habit. I now believe that he didn't actually like me.

I think he liked the stability I gave him.

I think he liked the lifestyle I maintained.

But me? He seemed to only tolerate.

He didn't worry about bills; I handled them. He'd say he "did what he could," as if doing *something sometimes* should count the same as being consistent.

He didn't carry most of the parenting load; I did. I managed school activities, haircuts, IEP meetings, volunteering. He'd conditioned the kids to believe that my standards were too high and that I was the problem. So there was little to no accountability on his part. I became the enemy for expecting excellence while he coasted.

The house was deteriorating around us, and I carried the weight of keeping it all from falling apart. When I asked for help, he'd deflect, telling me to "just get the kids to help" while he sat and did nothing.

When I left, he flipped the script and played the victim masterfully.

He told anyone who would listen, including my children, that I was the villain. That I'd had an affair (which I did). That I was selfish, cold, and abandoning the family.

What he didn't tell them was how deeply he had abandoned me—emotionally, financially, and physically—for years.

He didn't mention how, when I asked why he wouldn't touch me, he blamed my weight. As if he hadn't also gained eighty pounds and stopped trying entirely.

We both knew it was over.

When I finally told him I was leaving, there was no fight. No grand declaration. Just acceptance.

We agreed to remain friends for the sake of the kids.

Another manipulation.

Soon after, he stopped honoring our divorce decree, especially the financial obligations. He got fired again and left me holding the bag, this time with nearly $900 a month in medical expenses for one of our son's medications. Expenses I had to cover alone.

After taking on this unexpected expense, I refused to give him money for a toll pass account that we jointly had. I had to use the toll roads to get to my new job (the one that let me cover those extra bills). He retaliated. He called and reported the pass "lost/stolen"—without telling me. He'd rather I rack up fines than pay it himself because "you can afford it more than me."

He'd kept the car in the divorce, but as the primary borrower, my name was still on the loan.

He made the majority of the remaining payments thirty-plus days late.

He kept doing "what he could," and I kept doing *whatever it took.*

I hovered, micromanaged, and overcompensated, especially during my parenting weeks. I was tired of being both the good guy and the bad guy. Of always having to course-correct what he'd neglected.

He was right about one thing: I did do too much.

But it wasn't because I was overbearing. It was because I was terrified.

I was afraid my children would inherit the same identity wounds that I had. Rooted in abandonment, confusion, and low self-worth.

It was also because I was always on the hook for picking up the pieces.

Yes, I was controlling at times. Looking back now, I understand why.

I was exhausted. I was human.

And I didn't deserve what he gave me.

What I now understand is that he seemed to want me to remain where *he* saw me, not where I was or where I was headed.

Some of the labels I carried in that marriage—"too much," "selfish," "hard to love"—weren't my beliefs about myself. I think they were *his.*

They were projected onto me the moment I began breaking away.

It was time to break up with those labels too.

It was time to name what was really going on.

It wasn't just a divorce.

It was a declaration of freedom and redemption.

Pause & Reflect

When the Labels Aren't Yours to Carry

I didn't see it at the time.

But I wasn't just in a toxic relationship; I was contributing to it.

Not because I was malicious.

But because I was unhealed.

I thought love meant doing whatever it took to keep everything from falling apart.

Even when "everything" included *me*.

Here's what I now understand:

- **I was a big part of the problem.**

  Not by being abusive, but by staying too long, overfunctioning, ignoring my instincts, and allowing someone else's limitations to shape my life.

  Where have you mistaken endurance for wisdom?

- **Give yourself grace for your bad decisions and negative contributions.**

  You're not just the things you regret. You're also the one who had the courage to face them.

  Where do you need to forgive yourself for who you were while you were surviving?

- **Your partner is the single most important relationship you will choose.**

  It will either be a foundation or a fracture.

  And you will feel the ripple of that choice in every other area of your life.

  What kind of partner are you choosing, and what does that say about how you see yourself?

This wasn't just the end of a marriage.

It was the end of my complicity in my own suffering.

I didn't just leave *him*.

I left the version of me that accepted less than the truth of who I am.

V

CHASMS IN THE FOUNDATION

I was happy in my new spaces—physical, spiritual, and mental. I'd won a tremendous battle the day I chose to leave my marriage. But what I hadn't yet grasped was that this was just the opening salvo.

The war ahead wasn't with him.

It was with everyone else who thought they had a claim on my time, my voice, my labor—and most of all, with me.

I'd poured so much of my exhaustion into the disappointment of that broken marriage, assuming that once I left, the heaviness would lift. But the truth?

The weight wasn't just about him. It was embedded in nearly *every* relationship I had.

Role after role, I was the one holding the rope. The one filling the gaps. The one absorbing the weight . . . Daughter. Sister. Ex-wife. Mother. Relative. Colleague. Friend.

The toxicity hadn't ended with my husband. It just became more visible without him in the way.

Somewhere along the way, I had become the default solution.

If not the answer, then the bridge.

If not the bridge, then the glue.

Subconsciously, I'd trained everyone, and myself, to treat me like the power source. And like any overused battery, I was dying . . . quietly, steadily, and faster than normal.

People closest to me would ask for my advice or input, only to argue with me about it.

They weren't really asking. They were outsourcing their thinking and then resenting me for not cosigning their preferred narrative.

I started to question if my voice even mattered, or if it was only tolerated when it was convenient.

Leaving my husband sparked something. Journaling amplified it.

And soon enough, I found myself in a different kind of fight:

One with people who were deeply committed to their version of who I was *supposed* to be.

They were unrelenting. Some responded to my silence with anger. Others masked their manipulation as concern.

I remember one specific day, I was overwhelmed and exhausted, needed to set a boundary. I told one person:

"Today, I need me more than you need me."

Their reply?

"You're being selfish. I never ask you for anything."

(That was a lie. But at the time, I didn't even know how to name it as such.)

That moment made me pause and ask myself:

How had I ended up in relationships where my depletion was expected and my boundaries were optional?

Relationships where *my purpose* had become *my sacrifice?*

I told myself things like:

"God made me strong enough to carry this."

"This is my assignment."

"This is why I'm here."

But looking back now, I can see the distortion in that thinking.

Imagine being so detached from your own worth that you believe your highest calling is to be drained, daily, for people who won't even offer reciprocity for what you give so freely.

My relationship with myself didn't have cracks. It had chasms.

And from those chasms, I kept building connections that mirrored the void inside me.

Once I realized that, I stopped trying to create new relationships altogether.

At least not until I was whole. Not until I could build from a place of truth, not trauma.

And that's when I began drawing the lines.

Boundaries, not walls.

But real, firm, *non-negotiable* boundaries.

The kind that someone who truly loves herself would set.

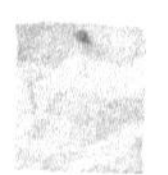

Pause & Reflect

When the Battle Was Me

I thought I left the war when I left the marriage.

But the real war?

It was internal.

It was about choosing myself—not just once, but every day after.

I thought I was walking into peace.

Instead, I was walking into the battlefield of everyone else's expectations . . . and finally confronting my own.

Here's what I know now:

- **My toxic relationship with myself was informed by my childhood.**

  I didn't just learn to survive in dysfunction; I learned to normalize it.

  I became the fixer because I was praised for being useful. I became the answer because I wasn't taught to ask for help.

  How did your earliest lessons teach you to love others more than yourself?

- **This was a literal fight for *my* life. Not the life others saw for me.**

  Not the daughter. Not the friend. Not the savior.

  But the woman beneath it all. The one who needed to matter *to herself.*

Whose version of "you" have you been trying to protect at your own expense?

- **Healing me first was the only way forward.**

  I couldn't build healthy love from broken foundations.

  I had to stop pretending I was okay while bleeding out in service to everyone else's comfort.

  What part of your healing have you been putting off until others get on board?

I wasn't being selfish.
I was being sovereign.

And sovereignty doesn't require permission.

VI

FUCK THIS SHIT—I'M OUT (THIRD TIME'S THE CHARM)

I'd been accidentally punishing myself for a long time. Not because I made intentionally harmful decisions.

Not because I deserved bad outcomes.

Not because of "karma."

No, my punishment came from not knowing how to lead my life with self-love as the primary guide.

I didn't trust my own voice. I didn't even *know* it.

So I listened to everyone else . . . about me.

And while it's true that I wasn't raised to understand self-trust, at some point, I made a decision . . .

I would become *completely* responsible for me.

This chapter marked that decision.

It was another **violent interruption** of a lifelong pattern of self-disregard and validation-seeking.

I was done.

Done with fighting to be seen.

Done with explaining myself.

Done with begging people to treat me the way I treated them.

Done with being the only one in the room who didn't think I deserved love, peace, or ease.

Imagine . . .

Facing the fact that the cracks in your closest relationships weren't just surface fractures—but deep chasms.

Imagine doing that while still reeling from the quiet trauma of spousal neglect and years of spiritual starvation.

Imagine realizing the confidence you'd projected for decades was just a polished mask—and inside, you were shaking.

Still standing. But not rooted.

Now imagine trying to set boundaries for the first time, with people who'd long relied on your silence.

Fighting to believe you deserved peace.

Fighting for your *own* attention.

That's where I was.

I wasn't in a death spiral—a vortex of sorts.

Years of momentum behind patterns that hadn't yet destroyed me, but would if I didn't change something *fast*.

Then came February.

The first year of the pandemic.

I started having sudden headaches—sharp, persistent, and unfamiliar.

One day, I ducked into a local grocery store and checked my blood pressure.

165/96.

WHAT. THE. WHAT?!

I'd lost weight. I was eating clean. I was meditating, praying, journaling.

I was doing everything *right* . . .

So how was this happening?

My doctor suggested anxiety.

Prescribed a common anti-anxiety med. Told me to come back in three months to determine if I also needed high blood pressure medication.

I nodded. Took the script. Drove home.

But something clicked.

I looked at the bottle and thought, *"These fools are literally going to kill me."*

I wasn't just physically tired; I was **soul tired**.

Tired of being the emotional mule.

Tired of people fighting me about *me*.

Tired of justifying my boundaries, my standards, my rest, my right to exist with peace.

And right then, I decided:

I wasn't going to take that damn medication.

Instead, I was going to change the **circumstances** that made it seem necessary.

Period.

That choice flipped a switch.

Suddenly, my tolerance was at zero for:

- Family members weaponizing guilt to access me.
- An ex-husband manipulating me through shared parenting logistics.
- Kids challenging my standards, because they'd been trained to think I was "too much."

No more.

Leaving the home I shared with my ex-husband had helped.

Now, I needed to leave **the whole environment**.

So I did what I'd done before.

I pivoted. Boldly. Sharply. Completely.

I announced that I was moving from my hometown to **Las Vegas**.

That summer.

Not just to find more sunshine.

But to **protect my peace**.

To walk away from the vortex.

To start over on my terms, in my voice, and in my time.

Because if this was going to be my life, then I was finally going to live it as *mine*.

Pause & Reflect

When the Power Returns to You

This wasn't just a decision to move across the country.

It was a declaration.

Of agency.

Of self-worth.

Of sovereignty.

For years, I'd been handing out pieces of myself like they were on clearance.

My time, my energy, my identity, my voice.

I thought I was being loving.

Supportive.

Strong.

What I was really being . . . was erased.

It took therapy to help me name what was happening.

It took courage to face the damage those patterns caused.

And it took everything I had left to stop handing my life over in the name of being "good," "selfless," or "useful."

Here's what I know now:

- **I didn't realize how much power I'd given over to other people until I was fighting to get it back.**

  When you're always the reliable one, people forget you're human.

  Sometimes, *you* forget you're human too.

  Where have you quietly surrendered your power without even realizing it?

- **I wouldn't have been able to identify the truths of what was happening without a lot of therapy.**

  When survival becomes your baseline, dysfunction feels normal.

  I needed help unpacking the noise—so I could finally hear *me*.

  What truths are waiting beneath your coping?

- **I wouldn't have been able to face and change those truths without a lot of courage.**

  Naming the problem is one thing.

  Walking away from everything familiar? That's another.

  What familiar dysfunction have you been too afraid to let go of?

- **This would be the last time I ever needed to fight for control of me.**

  I'm not asking for space anymore.

  I'm taking it.

  And I don't need anyone's permission to breathe freely ever again.

This wasn't a breakdown.
It was a reclamation.

And it was right on time.

VII

RIGHT REASON, WRONG DECISION

Let's be clear:

The reason I gave myself, and my family, for moving out of state was complete bullshit.

At the time, I was only about halfway through the inner work of identifying my self-destructive habits. That meant there was still plenty of room for those habits to creep back in, disguised as purpose. Comfort. Duty. I didn't recognize them as old crutches then, but looking back, that's exactly what they were. Familiar patterns and false anchors.

A family member needed some help, at least from what I was assessing. And just like that, Captain Nicole re-emerged, ready to rescue, to fix, to save.

I told myself (and everyone else) that I was moving away because I could be useful.

That my presence would make a difference.

That I was needed.

What I really was . . . was back in my "bootleg god" bag.

Still performing the same role I'd always played: the one who shows up and over-functions until she breaks.

And once again, my arrogance handed me a lesson I didn't want but absolutely needed.

This would be the last time I needed it.

Moving out of state was like jumping out of the frying pan and straight into the fire.

And it wasn't just the heat.

The pain from my own unresolved family issues in Chicago, combined with the chaos I stepped into, was the perfect storm for self-betrayal. Again.

The good news? I was a fighter. I knew how to pivot. I could bend circumstances to my will. I could push through tough things to get results . . . clean, organized, effective results.

The bad news? Those results were still coming at the cost of my peace.

The good news? Removing myself from Chicago was a necessary rupture. I needed a shock to the system. That move broke the pattern of everyday expectations people had of me—and more importantly, that I had of myself.

The bad news? I changed my environment without changing my insides. I brought my same need to be needed, my same unhealed identity, and planted it in even more unstable soil.

The good news? I did create real impact. I was able to help family a bit and work in the community. Even if only for a short while.

The bad news? No matter how much I gave, it would never be enough. Not for them. Not for me. Because I was still looking for external validation to affirm something only I could declare: I am enough.

I was still operating from the lie that usefulness equals worthiness.

And once again, I found myself in a familiar place: doing too much for people who couldn't, or wouldn't, reciprocate.

But here's what was different this time:

I was starting to hear my own voice.

Not just faintly, but clearly.

And this time, I was listening.

Which meant a new chapter was on the horizon.

One where I would choose to experience love toward me as someone's actions.

One where another physical plucking would be on the horizon.

Different than the rest, this time, the result would be the beginning of restoration.

Pause & Reflect

When Rescuing Is Actually Running in Disguise

I said I was moving to help.

I said it was about family.

I said they needed me.

But what I didn't say, what I couldn't admit at the time, was that I was also running.

Running from the mess I'd just escaped.

Running from the truth I hadn't fully accepted.

Running from the stillness that would force me to face myself.

Here's what I now understand:

- **My move out of state was as much about running away as it was about helping.**

  I packaged it as purpose, but it was part panic.

  I wasn't ready to sit with the truth of what I was still enduring despite leaving the marriage.

  So I threw myself into a new fire and called it duty.

  Where are you running while calling it service?

- **I was an unconscious glutton for punishment.**

  I didn't know how to not be used.

  Didn't know who I was without a crisis to fix.

  I wore usefulness like a badge, but really, it was a chain.

What have you mistaken for love that was actually self-betrayal?

- **The patterns I needed to interrupt were more internal than I realized.**

  It wasn't just about leaving places or people.

  It was about facing the parts of me that thought I didn't deserve peace unless I earned it.

  What pattern are you still repeating that you've dressed up as a virtue?

  I thought I could rescue others into healing.

But moving away showed me, again, that I was the one who needed saving.

And this time, it had to come from me letting my walls down enough to be cared for.

VIII

RESCUED (FROM MYSELF): AN ADULT INTRODUCTION TO PROTECTION

I met him in late May 2018, six months after I moved into my new house. I'd downloaded a dating app, mostly out of curiosity, and he was the first person I met up with from it.

Even before I saw him, I felt his presence enter the restaurant. There was an energy—strong, grounded, self-assured. He moved with intention. His purpose was clear, and everything about him conveyed it. He wasn't boastful, but he didn't shrink either. That night at dinner, it quickly became clear that I'd never been in personal proximity to that kind of alpha energy in a man, not in that way, not in my life.

We had easy conversation, the kind where time disappears. I assumed he was like other men I'd known . . . passive, dismissive, or uninterested in depth. Either afraid of who I was or uninterested in knowing more. Midway through dinner, he paused, looked me directly in the eye, and said, "Woman, you don't know who I am. I will buy another house and move you and your kids to Texas with me."

Oops.

Whatever assertiveness I had walked in with had just been met, and matched. I liked it. I craved it. And I immediately started subconsciously preparing to run from it.

He knew exactly who he wanted me to be to him: his wife. He came on strong. It was overwhelming. I was barely divorced, still rebuilding myself, trying to reclaim my voice and restore my sense of direction. I needed space. I needed air. I needed time.

So we dated for a few months, then let it go.

He gave me room.

We stayed in touch over the years. I'd call to check in, find a reason to stay connected, sometimes even ask for help. Every time, he picked up. Every time, he was kind, consistent, clear. The same steady presence. And though we weren't together, I now realize that he'd already shown me who he was. That very first night, when he claimed a vision of a life that included me and my children . . . I let him. I allowed that imprint to stay with me.

By spring 2020, I was planning the move out of state. And even though we weren't in a relationship, I intentionally didn't tell him. I knew he'd challenge me. I knew I'd listen. Something in me already knew this wasn't just a relocation but a regression.

Moving away, as I've shared, was chaos wrapped in duty. By winter of that year, I was deep in exhaustion and denial. I needed help, though I wasn't saying that out loud. He could feel it anyway. Something in my voice, though I thought I sounded fine, betrayed the truth.

He called me out.

He was furious that I hadn't asked for help, that I'd let myself spiral silently. And then he paid my rent. No strings. No expectations. Just care. The only thing he wanted for me was for me to be okay.

It was disorienting. I had spent years living in self-neglect. Suddenly, someone was not only being a soft place to land but was also holding me accountable for not treating myself better. He showed up, again. And this time, I didn't run. I leaned in.

But leaning in wasn't just about allowing someone else to love me. It was about doing the work to finally believe I was lovable.

Over the next year, I was healing in real time. I deepened my therapy. I spent more time journaling, praying, listening. I began identifying the pieces of me still living in hyper-vigilance. I stopped giving all my energy to external rescue missions and redirected it toward inner renovation. I started to challenge every thought that told me I wasn't ready, wasn't worthy, wasn't safe in softness.

By spring of 2021, we were officially dating again.

That April and May, he spent most of his time in the other state with me. I was still trying to support family, serve the church I'd joined, and hold everything together. He supported me through it all. But something about his energy highlighted the imbalance I'd normalized.

He asked questions, loving but pointed, about how much I was giving and what I was receiving. I kept offering reflexive justifications. He never demanded that I change, but he didn't cosign the chaos either. Eventually, his tolerance for the dysfunction wore thin. He remained emotionally present, but began to step back from the physical mess. Without saying the words, he was drawing a line: "I will love you through this, but I won't live in this."

And then, true to the vision he'd shared on our first date, he went home to Texas and fast-tracked the completion of the house he'd bought in 2019. A house big enough for all of our kids. A house he'd always intended for us. When it was ready, he presented options. Stay in disorder, or step into a different kind of life.

He wasn't rescuing me. He was inviting me.

And this time, I was ready to say yes.

By early June 2021, after my niece's high school graduation, he packed and shipped most of my belongings from where I was to Texas. He packed the rest in the car with me and my teenage children. Then he drove us eighteen hours across state lines to a home, our home, that he had made ready.

That move wasn't just about geography.

It was a spiritual relocation.

The woman who stepped out of that car wasn't the same woman who had packed it.

This time, I wasn't running from something.

I was stepping fully into something I chose.

My foundation was being reset, because I was finally willing to believe I deserved solid ground.

Pause & Reflect

When Love Doesn't Have to Hurt

I used to think love had to be hard.

That it required proving.

That it demanded suffering.

That if it didn't hurt a little, maybe it wasn't real.

But what I learned . . .

And what I'm still learning is that healthy love holds you without squeezing you dry.

It doesn't shout to be heard.

It doesn't vanish when you're messy.

It shows up, over and over again.

Here's what I know now:

- **Love is demonstrated in support, patience, kindness, discipline, and action.**

  Not just words. Not just vibes.

  Real love shows up with presence. With groceries. With rent money. With packed boxes and long drives.

  Who in your life has shown up in the quiet but sacrificial ways?

- **I always deserved a healthy love from everyone, not just my future husband.**

  I had accepted scraps and called it normal.

  But love, true love, doesn't ask you to shrink or settle. It lifts and aligns.

Where in your life have you mistaken survival for love?

- **I had to learn how to be loved in a healthy way.**

  Because even when it showed up, I didn't recognize it at first.

  Healthy love felt foreign. Softness felt unsafe.

  Learning to receive love required unlearning what I thought love required of me.

  What old beliefs about love are you ready to release?

This wasn't just about meeting the right partner.

This was about becoming the kind of woman who could be fully seen, held, and loved, because she finally believed she was worthy of all three.

IX

RECONNECTING IN CHICAGO

Life was still a whirlwind, but for the first time, the spiral was upward. I was finally catching air in a vortex that had once threatened to swallow me whole. My personal development work was helping me to finally loosen the grip of a lifelong pull of trauma, obligation, and repeated patterns of self-betrayal.

I'd done meaningful work by then. I'd named my wounds, redefined my relationships, set boundaries that cost me, but also kept me. Still, something was missing. I wasn't yet *living* from those new beliefs.

Because the truth? I didn't yet trust them. They were unfamiliar.

I didn't know how to live without waiting for the next hit. I didn't know how to feel joy without bracing for disappointment. I didn't know how to *just be*, not producing anything, not fixing anything, not apologizing for anything. Just present . . . worthy . . . whole.

I didn't know how to believe I deserved peace without guilt clawing at my back.

Even with boundaries in place, I struggled. Guilt for setting them. Fear that my children might see me as selfish. Pain from knowing that my ex-husband had spent years undermining my efforts, trying to turn them against me, while doing very little to move them forward himself.

That added to my paranoia.

I'd worked so hard to show my kids what strength and love looked like. And here he was, eroding that work with careless words and absent actions. I was shocked. Then I was furious. Then I was *done* letting someone else's behavior define how I saw myself.

Their perception of me, anyone's, really, could no longer determine the way I chose to care for myself. Their resentment, their judgments, their discomfort with my growth? That was their work, not mine.

It didn't mean the pain vanished. It meant I finally knew where to place it.

Another layer peeled back: the one where I had centered everyone else's needs and feelings above my own. This time, I let the tears come. The guttural, ugly ones. The kind that sting your face while physically forcing the truth out of your body.

And that truth? I deserved the same care I poured into everyone else. I had to hold others accountable for treating me with the same intention and grace I extended to them.

This work, this recalibration, would stretch over the next year . . . still being worked on today.

I continued to write constantly. Journaling remained my mirror and compass, helping me realign my voice with the healed version of myself I was still becoming. I started inching back toward the family I had once distanced myself from. But I didn't want to return the same way I left.

I had to come back with boundaries rooted in love, not resentment. I had to train *myself* first in how to honor my voice. Only then could I teach others how to respect it too.

But I wondered: *Were they ready for the version of me I was bringing back?*

In protecting myself, I had broken some trust. Severed ties without warning. Left people feeling abandoned. The way I left may have been necessary for my survival, but the way I returned had to be rooted in integrity.

So, in the fall of 2022, I bought a home back in the old neighborhood. Not to regress, but to repair. I wanted to rebuild trust, mine and theirs. To only live from the healthiest version of myself. To lead relationships from a place of inner stability, where my needs weren't invisible and my boundaries weren't negotiable.

Conversations became more honest. Connections more intentional. I learned to offer grace without self-erasure, and to listen without losing myself.

I wasn't perfect. I never will be.

But this . . . this was the most whole I had ever felt. And that wholeness was mine to keep.

Pause & Reflect

When Accountability Becomes a Form of Love

For a long time, I thought healing was just about being heard.

Being seen.

Being validated for the pain I'd carried and survived.

And it is.

But it's also about being honest, brutally honest, about the parts I played too.

Not to erase my pain.

But to reclaim my power.

Here's what I know now:

- **Yes, I was a victim, but at times I was a villain.**

  I've run when I could've stayed.

  I've lashed out when I could've paused.

  I've hidden behind silence and self-righteousness when clarity and courage were required.

  And none of that negates the ways I was also deeply wounded.

  What parts of your story still need your accountability as much as your compassion?

- **I had to be accountable for how I contributed to the situations.**

  Even when I was operating from exhaustion.

  Even when I had the best intentions.

  Even when I thought I was doing the right thing.

Harm is harm, even when it's wrapped in justification.

Where might your impact have hurt someone, even if you didn't mean to?

- **Ownership for the changed relationships started with my changed relationship with myself.**

  The truth is: I had to face me first.

  I had to own how many times I abandoned myself before I ever addressed who else had.

  The way I restored relationships wasn't by apologizing first to them; it was by telling the truth to me.

  What would it look like to rebuild your relationships from a place of radical self-respect?

This wasn't just about making peace with others.

It was about making peace with my patterns.

Because healing doesn't just give you your voice back.

It hands you a mirror and asks if you're finally ready to see the whole picture.

DEAR READER: FINAL THOUGHTS . . .

Writing this book was cathartic for me in so many ways. Each of the above sections represents a tiny snippet of the substance of the era of time it represents. Each of the section headings is the title of some other written work I've started. Some of those works I started well over ten years ago.

One of the first public speaking opportunities I had was given to me by a church pastor over twelve years ago. It was for a women's day event, and each speaker was charged with identifying a historically significant woman and speaking about her.

I didn't want to do one of the names that everyone always knew, so I found a woman whose story resonated with my spirit. It was the story of the female founder of a successful chain of stores.

She'd experienced a traumatic event in a place that was supposed to present her with an opportunity. Her response to that trauma caused her to make some unconventional decisions for someone from her background at the time. In living through those decisions, she would ultimately find herself separated from her partner and needing to make a way to care for her family.

The products that she sold to meet her family's needs turned into a global brand that many of us shop at today.

I titled this talk "Pain ~ Purpose ~ Promise."

This woman had experienced a painful event. Her response to that event caused her to enter several processes from which she would create part of her life's purpose. In pursuit of that purpose, she began living in the external promises of life available to her.

You've spent some time reading through these same themes in my life. The trauma in my life started early. My responses to those traumatic events caused me to enter processes that would lead me to writing this book that you're reading today. As I pursue sharing my story in hopes of empowering you to live yours, I too will add to the levels of promise that I'm already experiencing.

Read the book; take the lessons; examine yourself; free yourself; find the courage to live in the promises available to your life.

The world is waiting for you!

Yours in courage,
Nicole

EPILOGUE: THE PRESENT AND REALIZATION

I've always been one to work on myself. My motivation for being better has always been innate. I've also always attached to people (older women in particular) who would help pull the best out of me. The only way that I survived these experiences while maintaining the vibrant and resilient spirit that I have today is because of the people who were around me.

Whether family, friend, or mentor, I always had this amazing balance of positive influences to offset the negative chaos. These were people who would let me vent or bounce my thoughts off of them. They were also people who would hold my hand when I was distraught or hold me accountable when I was wrong.

When I walked into therapy, I walked in thinking that I was the problem and I needed to be fixed. When I walked out of therapy a little under two years later, I walked out knowing that my primary problem was that I didn't love or respect myself enough. I'm far from perfect, but I didn't deserve what was happening to me.

I would spend the next few years both facing and embracing myself—flaws, forgiveness, and all.

The following pages contain a few of the most powerful processes that I had to take myself through in order to know myself and trust me with me.

Acknowledgment I: Life as it was happening wasn't working for me anymore.

At some point, I realized life as I was living it just wasn't working anymore.

Looking back, I'd been soaking in toxicity most of my life. Like a teabag left too long in boiling water, I'd absorbed the bitterness around me until it flavored my entire existence.

On the surface, I understood the concept of self-worth. But my lived experience told me a different story. The messages I'd absorbed since childhood said I wasn't worthy of protection, that I mattered the least.

To maintain my natural joy, I learned to tie my self-acceptance to other people's happiness. Pleasing them became my currency for belonging. Their smiles became my mirror. From the outside, it looked fine. I had a good family, good jobs, progressive goals. But none of it was really mine. I wasn't chasing my own joy; I was chasing their joy in my outcomes.

Now, when I achieve something, it's sweeter—because I know it's for me.

Courage: *I identified the areas that I didn't like and began working to change them.*

Once I acknowledged the truth, I had to start changing it. And that required me to face myself.

I had to admit that I didn't want to be so strong all the time. I didn't want to always be the one with the answers. I had gained almost a hundred pounds. I wasn't happy with myself . . . inside or out. I was constantly fighting for or against something, never at peace, always in survival mode.

And the hardest truth? I'd done it to myself.

Yes, I was trained that way. But there came a point when the choices were mine. I had made myself the hero in the stories of too many other people. And if I had gotten myself here, then I was the only one who could get myself out.

With the help of my village, I started peeling back the layers. They let me be vulnerable. They let me admit my fears and insecurities. But they also held up mirrors when I needed correction. It was equal parts grace and accountability, and exactly what I needed.

The Reversal Process: *A flaming hot mess of confusion (and yes, that's my professional diagnosis).*

Resetting expectations with everyone around me was a messy and necessary process.

Some days it looked like me crying in my car after a conversation because I couldn't believe I'd actually said out loud what I needed. Other days it was me in a full-blown argument, voice shaking but determined not to back down from the boundary I knew I had to set. It was signing divorce papers with tears in my eyes, knowing it was necessary but still feeling like I was failing. I was awkwardly distancing myself from old friends who no longer fit, while stumbling my way into new circles that challenged me to grow.

I journaled furiously during this time. The pages were filled with half-thoughts, ugly confessions, and desperate prayers. It was the only way I knew how to find myself. I leaned heavily on mentors who pushed me to retrain my thinking. Slowly but surely, I built new boundaries with myself and others.

With every new boundary came a wave of guilt. Sadness. The feeling that I was betraying the people who had counted on me to stay the same. Sometimes I even caught myself wondering if I was selfish, or worse, sanctimonious—crossing oceans for people who wouldn't cross the street for me and then calling it love.

But here's what the mess eventually helped me understand: They were never my responsibility.

I wasn't saving them. They were committed to whatever they were committed to. And I was **definitely not** saving me.

So, I stopped.

Acknowledgment II: I'd internalized a litany of limiting beliefs about myself.

Limiting beliefs are "perceptions and thoughts you have about yourself, others, and the world. And they're self-limiting because these perceptions and thoughts are preventing you from doing something that you're actually quite capable of doing (even though you don't think you are!)" —*Psychology Today*

My limiting beliefs operated with the cross-functional efficiency of a Fortune 500 company; i.e., they worked very well together. So well, in fact, that I had trouble specifically identifying the beliefs on an individual basis.

They were interconnected like a thousand-piece jigsaw puzzle of Nicole. A puzzle that had just been opened and dumped onto the table before scattering the pieces all out so you could try to make sense of which pieces went where.

Here are the strongest of the limiting beliefs that I had to work through:

On Self-Worth

- I'm not good enough.
- Good things don't last.
- People don't care about me.
- I have to earn love.

These beliefs kept me chasing acceptance outside of myself, instead of believing I was worthy just as I was.

On Money and Opportunity

- Success is for people who don't look like me.
- Rich people are evil.
- "They" will always find a way to take from me.
- Struggling is normal. It's what I'm supposed to do.
- Hustling is the only way to survive.

I believed money and opportunity were always on the other side of a door I wasn't allowed to open.

On Safety and Trust

- Nobody is safe for me—not even me.
- I'm always at risk and powerless.
- Strength is the only acceptable response to every situation.

These scripts taught me to armor up, even when what I needed was protection or comfort.

On Ability

- No matter how hard I work, it will never be enough.

This one sentence kept me grinding, striving, proving—yet never resting in what I had already accomplished.

On Race

- The world is only two cultures: Black and White.
- White people want to discard Black people.
- Black people want to discard Black people.
- I'm too Black to be accepted in professional circles.
- I'm too White to be accepted in Black social circles.
- Black people have to fight for everything.

I lived in between, carrying the weight of not feeling "enough" for either side.

On Relationships

- Love hurts.
- Intentions matter more than outcomes.
- Breaking boundaries is normal in relationships.
- Setting boundaries makes me think I'm better than others.
- Fighting is normal.

These beliefs left me excusing harm, shrinking my needs, and confusing dysfunction with intimacy.

On Healing and Evolution

- My healing will disrupt everyone else—and that's not fair to them.
- God made me strong so I can carry it all for other people.

Even healing felt like a burden. I thought becoming whole meant betraying the people who needed my brokenness.

Courage: *Identify those specific beliefs and begin to confront them.*

Sometimes the hardest person to hold accountable is yourself. It's easier to look outward. To look at what people did that they shouldn't have, or what they failed to do that they should have and call it the reason for your pain. And to be fair, my entire life experience up until that point had reaffirmed every limiting belief I carried.

But staying in that space was a powerless position. And if there's one thing I cannot stand, it's feeling powerless. The only way I knew to take my power back was to turn the mirror on myself and ask: What part did I play?

There were moments when I had no control and life just happened. But even then, how I responded shaped where I ended up later. I couldn't hold myself accountable for what was beyond me, but I could absolutely own how I reacted, how I showed up, and how I allowed myself to stay in certain patterns.

That takes an immense amount of courage. And for me, it specifically looked like:

- Admitting that I stayed in relationships long after I knew they were harmful.
- Owning the ways I overextended myself to "be the hero" because I was addicted to being needed.

- Facing the truth that I muted my voice in rooms where I should have spoken up *(because silence felt safer than confrontation).*
- Accepting that chasing validation from others was my way of avoiding the harder work of validating myself.

Every time I named one of those truths, I felt both the sting of honesty and the relief of reclaiming power. Accountability didn't mean blaming myself for everything; it meant refusing to live as if I had no choice.

And that shift changed everything.

The Reversal Process: *The flamin' hot mess of confusion (cont.)*

The work of confronting my limiting beliefs was emotionally raw and unpleasant. They didn't show up as a tidy list . . . I had to catch them in real time, usually disguised as self-doubt: *You don't matter. You'll never be enough. Success isn't for people like you.*

So I started to actively catch myself in the act. In any given moment, I forced myself to pause and pay attention to the emotions I was feeling. Instead of pushing them aside, I acknowledged them and asked:

- What exactly am I feeling?
- What is this belief trying to tell me?
- Is it even true?

Journaling remained my lifeline in this process. Some days the expressions were clear and sharp; other days they were messy, angry, scared . . . some of them even ugly. I let them come. I gave myself permission to write whatever surfaced, then I examined those words and calibrated them against my truth. The ones that resonated stayed. The ones that didn't, I got rid of and kept digging until I uncovered what did.

Through this practice, I began to know myself. I didn't fully trust myself yet, but I was training myself to *hear* my own voice. And once I found that voice, I started listening differently to the conversations I was having with me.

The beliefs were never polite enough to announce themselves directly—they crept in as hesitation, second-guessing, or the urge to seek constant validation. At the time, I thought I just needed a "sounding board."

In reality, I was exposing myself to me and my village. Sharing my thoughts and fears with people I trusted helped me recognize the lies I had internalized. Their love and accountability gave me the courage to keep facing them.

Acknowledgment III: I'd been misused by most of the people around me for most of my adult life.

Throughout my life, I've lived within many roles: daughter, sister, friend, student, employee, wife, mother, entrepreneur. Each came with titles, definitions, and expectations that felt both endearing and heavy with responsibility.

For a long time, I carried an idealistic picture of how these roles should look. Not just how I should perform in them, but how others should show up for me within them. And like so many of us, I was deeply influenced by cultural projections.

Commercials painted mothers and daughters as inseparable. Smiling through every exchange, sharing long phone calls, basking in love and satisfaction. Family units on TV showed husbands and wives who, even when they disagreed, always resolved things calmly, rationally, with little emotion.

Naturally, I thought: *That's how my life should look too.* No inner work, no self-awareness, no effort to consider how my behavior impacted others. Just show up, and—like magic—happiness would bloom.

Boy, was my awakening rude. It smacked my audacity right in the face. A full-on metaphysical assault.

The truth was sobering: I was in toxic relationships in nearly every role I played. Looking back, I can see how few boundaries existed, how much childhood trauma was bleeding into adult dynamics, and how unfair expectations shaped our interactions.

There I was, presenting myself as something I didn't have to be, filling gaps I didn't create and wasn't responsible for. And there they were, ready to let me do it. It was a complete misuse of me—primarily facilitated by me.

Courage: *Remove myself from the environment and begin to establish boundaries.*

As I became more conscious about my limiting beliefs, I gave myself no choice but to face them. I did not want to live a lie, no matter how uncomfortable the truth was.

Me confronting myself also meant confronting the relational patterns that I had with everyone around me. This work was neither quick nor easy.

It required a breaking of the bonds that were established in toxicity, including the biggest one with myself.

It's difficult to look yourself in the eye and specifically label the lies you've been living from.

It's even more difficult to decide to confront those lies, conquer them, and establish a new truth to live from.

However, none of this would have been as difficult as staying in a place that I wasn't designed to be in.

The Reversal Process: *A violent interruption of the pattern*

Some synonyms for violent, according to Webster:

1. extremely powerful or forceful and capable of causing damage
2. notably forceful, furious, or vehement
3. extreme, intense

What started as a drip campaign, me hinting to people that something had to change, over time became more direct, confrontational, sometimes even abrupt. My transformation felt necessary to me, but to those around me, it was jarring.

Everyone wasn't on the same journey. Still, we were all in relationship together, bound by longstanding patterns that had become familiar, even if not healthy. *Better the devil you know* seemed to be the unspoken rule. My decision to evolve didn't just affect me; it disrupted the balance they were used to. And the truth was, they hadn't signed up for that.

It became a decade-long battle over me: how I identified myself, how I showed up, and how my growth would inevitably demand that others show up differently too.

At first, I tried to ease the transition. I shared my doubts, my fears, my self-reflections—as though explaining and over-explaining might buy me permission to grow. I offered resources. Invited people to therapy, both for themselves and with me.

I clung to those relationships because I thought they were vital to my survival. I didn't want to let them go.

But breaking old habits, and sometimes breaking whole relationships, was brutal. My marriage ended in divorce. At times, I stopped communicating with my mother and sister. The final rupture came when I moved across the country during the pandemic, under the guise of "helping" family. In reality, I was using their need as an excuse to escape bonds I couldn't cut on my own.

The hardest truth? That move wasn't about them at all. It was about me still chasing validation, still feeding the savior complex I thought proved my worth.

What I finally had to face was violent in its own way: the realization that the life I'd been living, most of my adult life, was toxic to me.

Thirteen years into my healing journey, I knew it was time. Time to stop the destructive patterns. Time to stop rescuing everyone else.

Time, finally, to start being fair to me.

Acknowledgment IV: I would often place myself in other people's shadows.

Something that baffled me throughout my healing journey was how much weight people gave to my opinion. I never understood why my voice mattered so much to them.

This showed up especially when I started resetting boundaries. People would ask for my perspective, then argue with me when I gave it. I'd find myself thinking, *If you only want me to say what you want to hear, why ask me at all?* It felt like a trap.

I craved the freedom to say what I thought, honestly and directly, without carrying the responsibility of being anyone's "leading voice." What I preferred instead was to find someone else's platform and throw my energy behind them. I would lend my time, my knowledge, my skills, and my spirit of excellence to help others shine. In my mind, if I pushed them forward, I would rise naturally with them, but still remain in the background, where it felt safer.

I did this in so many ways. I aligned myself with a small graphic design company, pouring effort into helping an unqualified but talented owner try to build something sustainable. I volunteered for several churches, doing the behind-the-scenes work to move the mission forward. Each time, I convinced myself I was serving others. But if I'm honest, I was also hiding. Hiding from the creative responsibility of building something of my own. Hiding from the human obligation of letting people depend on me.

I hear my mother's voice even now: "Co-Co, your voice has so much more weight than you realize." And all I wanted in those moments was for people to **leave me alone**.

I wanted greatness, but from behind the curtain.

Courage: *Accept that I am enough and have been all along.*

The truth is that I was scared. I was scared of failure. I was also scared of success. I was constantly confronting imposter syndrome. I was working through the negative conversations from the "Committee of Self-Doubt" and their daily meetings in my head.

I'd been submerged in a pool of narcissistic abuse for nearly seventeen years (the marriage), and that was *after* all other trauma.

I believed the lies. I didn't believe in me.

I decided to change that.

The Reversal Process: *Believing the truth*

I remember when it hit me: It probably wasn't a good thing that I couldn't look myself in the eye.

Around that time, I had a mentor who encouraged us to do mirror talks. Boy, I couldn't even get through a full sentence. My eyes darted everywhere but back at me. I didn't believe a word coming out of my own mouth.

That realization didn't make sense, not with everything else I was learning about personal growth. So, I decided to change it. I started small, practicing in the visor mirror of my car at stoplights.

That was about all I could handle at first. It wasn't enough to tape affirmations to my mirror; I needed real conversations between me and me—the **real** me.

I confronted the broken version of myself. I challenged myself to speak life into my own eyes the same way I'd always spoken life into others when they were hurting. At first, the words were generic and common. But gradually, the conversation shifted. Instead of letting the "Committee of Self-Doubt" dictate the script, I began saying the exact opposite out loud.

The Bible says faith comes by hearing. For me, belief came when my ears heard my own voice. Slowly, I learned to borrow the belief others had in me until I was strong enough to believe for myself.

Belief grew into celebration. Celebration into confidence. Through this newly cleansed lens of self-reflection, I started to see myself clearly: I was actually pretty dope. I had accomplished so much despite everything life had thrown at me.

More than that, I had done it with integrity. Through failures, bumps, outside attacks, and even my own self-sabotage, I still managed to land on my feet. Even if the victory was only internal, I always rose. And I did it without losing my joy, my generosity, or my heart.

Acknowledgment V: I began to lean into my greatness.

By the end of 2022, I knew I was almost ready to "try again." I had done years of work and was finally on the tail end of it, but I also knew myself well enough to admit: I still had a flair for self-sabotage.

Yes, I was wounded. But I'm not a quitter. And really—what is life if you can't live it on your own terms?

Excelling had always been a part of my DNA. My mother taught me that if the stars were out there, I should at least try to touch them. She never raised me to settle, and for that I'll always be grateful.

But this time, I knew I had to be smarter about me. Instead of ignoring my lessons and hoping for the best, I chose to see life as it actually was—not just as I wished it to be. I made a conscious decision to bank on myself. Not simply because I knew how to survive, but because I had finally learned how to live. How to be.

I had learned to love myself—flaws and all.

I celebrated the wins.

I recalibrated from the losses.

I spoke from my spirit with boldness.

I lived with integrity and accountability.

I honored my boundaries and allowed others to honor theirs.

I became convinced of my own sufficiency—and I knew no one could take that from me again.

I AM ENOUGH.

Courage: *Make a plan and refuse to quit.*

I have over twenty years of professional experience across industries, building strategies, executing plans, and delivering results. But when it came to my own plans? I often stopped short.

Life's chaos and my own emotions would slow me down. Excuses came easy. "It's too much." "It won't work." "Maybe later." I knew this about myself, and in 2022, I was determined to face it head-on.

This time, I committed to holding myself accountable—not to my fears, not to my self-doubt, but to the greatest parts of me I can now see.

The Reversal Process: *Creating new neural pathways*

Growth meant retraining my mind and building new neural pathways that made thriving my default, not just surviving. I had lived long enough letting the "Committee of Self-Doubt" dictate my voice. Now, I was determined to practice a different truth until it felt like second nature:

That I am capable.

That I am resilient.

That I am worthy of the life I desire.

That I am ENOUGH.

CLOSING THE CIRCLE

My journey has been messy, beautiful, painful, and restorative. I've shared the cracks, the chasms, the breaks, and the rebuilding. I've shared the lies and the truths, the brokenness and the becoming.

Looking back, the three threads that run through everything I've written here are: **Pain, Purpose, and Promise**.

Pain: The losses, violations, and patterns that imprinted me with lies about my worth. The moments that silenced my voice or made me feel like I wasn't enough.

Purpose: The work of untangling those lies, finding my voice, building boundaries, and choosing to live consciously. Pain taught me to search deeper, and purpose gave me direction.

Promise: The life I now claim is one rooted in sufficiency, joy, and self-respect. Not a perfect life, but a whole one. A life where I know, beyond doubt: **I am enough**.

But this book isn't only about me—it's about you.

I invite you to look at your own life through the same lens:

Where has ***pain*** shaped the way you see yourself?

How might that pain be pointing you toward ***purpose***?

And what is the ***promise*** you can claim if you choose to unbecome what was never yours?

Your work, like mine, won't be neat. It won't always be pretty. But it will be worth it.

Healing isn't about becoming someone new . . . It's about unbecoming everything you never were until all that remains is the truest version of you.

YOU ARE ENOUGH

ABOUT THE AUTHOR

Nicole Lynn Morris is an author, speaker, and corporate leader who merges strategic precision with soul-level transformation. With more than twenty years of professional and leadership experience, she currently serves as a Senior Manager in the Healthcare space, leading cross-functional initiatives that simplify complexity and turn vision into measurable results.

Beyond corporate walls, Nicole is the **founder of Labels Be Gone**, a movement and forthcoming book series inviting readers to unlearn the identities that no longer serve them. Her debut memoir, *It's Not Me, It's You*, is a raw and redemptive act of reclamation—part storytelling, part mirror—that challenges readers to release who the world told them to be and remember who they are.

She also leads **The Ember Experience**, a reflective community built around conversation, healing, and permission to take up space. And through her ambassador work with **Love & Protect Wisdom**, a Chicago-based nonprofit, she supports initiatives that provide both immediate and long-term resources for victims of domestic violence.

An MBA graduate of Keller Graduate School of Management and certified PMP and CSM, Nicole brings together process expertise, emotional intelligence, and truth-telling to help individuals and organizations unlearn, re-label, and undo the damage of misplaced and limiting beliefs.

This book dared you to face the truth.

Now dare to *live* it.

Join **The Ember Experience**—a reflective space for anyone ready to unlearn the lies, release old labels, and live with unflinching authenticity.

It's where honest stories meet collective healing, and where you'll be reminded:

You were never too much. You were always enough. And now, you'll be beautifully becoming.

https://labesbegone.com
You're not alone in your journey of unbecoming.

The B Corp Movement

Dear reader,

Thank you for reading this book and joining the Publish Your Purpose community! You are joining a special group of people who aim to make the world a better place.

What's Publish Your Purpose About?

Our mission is to elevate the voices often excluded from traditional publishing. We intentionally seek out authors and storytellers with diverse backgrounds, life experiences, and unique perspectives to publish books that will make an impact in the world.

Beyond our books, we are focused on tangible, action-based change. As a woman- and LGBTQ+-owned company, we are committed to reducing inequality, lowering levels of poverty, creating a healthier environment, building stronger communities, and creating high-quality jobs with dignity and purpose.

As a Certified B Corporation, we use business as a force for good. We join a community of mission-driven companies building a more equitable, inclusive, and sustainable global economy. B Corporations must meet high standards of transparency, social and environmental performance, and accountability as determined by the nonprofit B Lab. The certification process is rigorous and ongoing (with a recertification requirement every three years).

How Do We Do This?

We intentionally partner with socially and economically disadvantaged businesses that meet our sustainability goals. We embrace and encourage our authors and employee's differences in race, age, color, disability, ethnicity, family or marital status, gender identity or expression, language, national origin, physical and mental ability, political affiliation, religion, sexual orientation, socio-economic status, veteran status, and other characteristics that make them unique.

Community is at the heart of everything we do—from our writing and publishing programs to contributing to social enterprise nonprofits like reSET (https://www.resetco.org/) and our work in founding B Local Connecticut.

We are endlessly grateful to our authors, readers, and local community for being the driving force behind the equitable and sustainable world we are building together.

To connect with us online, or publish with us,
visit us at www.publishyourpurpose.com.

Elevating Your Voice,

Jenn T Grace

Jenn T. Grace

Founder, Publish Your Purpose

www.ingramcontent.com/pod-product-compliance
Ingram Content Group UK Ltd.
Pitfield, Milton Keynes, MK11 3LW, UK
UKHW062256290726
14090UKWH00017B/714

9 798887 971919